THE GREAT COOKS' GUIDE TO

Ice Cream

& Other Frozen Desserts

GREAT COOKS' LIBRARY

America's leading food authorities share their home-tested
recipes and expertise on cooking equipment and techniques

THE GREAT COOKS' GUIDE TO

Ice Cream
& Other Frozen Desserts

A BEARD GLASER WOLF BOOK

RANDOM HOUSE, NEW YORK

Front Cover (left to right, top to bottom): Lemon Sherbet in Lemon Shells, page 32; Creamy Chocolate Ice Cream, page 22 *(ice cream mold courtesy Charles F. Lamalle).*

Back Cover (left to right, top to bottom): *(ice cream freezer courtesy Hammacher Schlemmer; ice cream bombe mold courtesy Charles F. Lamalle).*

Interior Photographs: Page 6, *thermometer courtesy The Professional Kitchen;* page 7, *ice cream freezer courtesy Hammacher Schlemmer;* page 9 (top), *ice cream freezer courtesy Waring Products;* page 10, *ice cream molds courtesy Charles F. Lamalle;* page 12 (top), *ice cream scoop courtesy H. Roth & Son, sherbet scoop courtesy The Professional Kitchen.*

Book Design by Milton Glaser, Inc.

Cover Photograph by Richard Jeffery

Food Styling by Lucy Wing
Props selected by Yvonne McHarg and Beard Glaser Wolf Ltd.

Library of Congress Cataloguing in Publication Data

Main entry under title:

The Great cooks guide to ice cream & other frozen desserts.
(The Great cooks' library)
1. Ice cream, ices, etc. 2. Desserts, Frozen. I. Series.
TX795.G84   641.8'62   77-17690
ISBN 0-394-73606-0

Manufactured in the United States of America
2 4 6 8 9 7 5 3
First Edition

We have gathered together some of the great cooks in this country to share their recipes—and their expertise—with you. As you read the recipes, you will find that in certain cases techniques will vary. This is as it should be: Cooking is a highly individual art, and our experts have arrived at their own personal methods through years of experience in the kitchen.

THE EDITORS

CONTRIBUTORS

Michael Batterberry, author of several books on food, art and social history, is also a painter, and is editor and food critic for a number of national magazines. He has taught at James Beard's cooking classes in New York and many of his original recipes have appeared in *House & Garden, House Beautiful* and *Harper's Bazaar.*

Bianca Brown, now a freelance food writer, has worked as associate food editor at *Good Housekeeping* writing the feature, "Foods with a Foreign Flavor," and as associate editor at *Gourmet* magazine.

Ruth Ellen Church, a syndicated wine columnist for the *Chicago Tribune*, had been food editor for that newspaper for more than thirty years when she recently retired. The author of seven cookbooks, her most recent books are *Entertaining with Wine* and *Wines and Cheeses of the Midwest.*

Elizabeth Schneider Colchie is a noted food consultant who has done extensive recipe development and testing as well as research into the history of foods and cookery. She was on the editorial staff of *The Cooks' Catalogue* and *The International Cooks' Catalogue* and has written numerous articles for such magazines as *Gourmet* and *Family Circle.*

Isabel S. Cornell, a home economist, was Associate Editor for the revised edition of *Woman's Day Encyclopedia of Cookery* and Special Projects Editor for the revised edition of *Woman's Day Collector's Cook Book*. While on the *Woman's Day* staff, she selected, tested and judged for their recipe contests.

Carol Cutler, who has been a food columnist for the *Washington Post*, is a graduate of the Cordon Bleu and l'Ecole des Trois Gourmands in Paris. She is the author of *Haute Cuisine for Your Heart's Delight* and *The Six-Minute Soufflé and Other Culinary Delights*. She has also written for *House & Garden, American Home* and *Harper's Bazaar*.

Florence Fabricant is a freelance writer, reporting on restaurants and food for *The New York Times, New York* magazine and other publications. She was on the staff of *The Cooks' Catalogue* and editor of the paperback edition. She also contributed to *The International Cooks' Catalogue* and *Where to Eat in America*.

Emanuel and Madeline Greenberg co-authored *Whiskey in the Kitchen* and are consultants to the food and beverage industry. Emanuel, a home economist, is a regular contributor to the food columns of *Playboy* magazine. Both contribute to *House Beautiful, Harper's Bazaar* and *Travel & Leisure*.

Mireille Johnston, the author of *The Cuisine of the Sun,* a cookbook of Provençal specialties, is currently completing a book on the cooking of Burgundy, *The Cuisine of the Rose*.

Alma Lach holds a Diplôme de Cordon Bleu from Paris and has served as food editor for the *Chicago Sun-Times*. She is author of *How's and Why's of French Cooking* and *Cooking à la Cordon Bleu* as well as many other cookbooks and articles on food. She directs the Alma Lach Cooking School in Chicago and is currently the television chef on the PBS program "Over Easy."

Jeanne Lesem, Family Editor of United Press International, is the author of *The Pleasures of Preserving and Pickling*.

Linda Lewis is co-founder of Miss Grimble's bakery in New York City and a consultant on new products, recipe development and menu planning to food companies and restaurants.

Susan Lipke is an Associate Editor of the Great Cooks' Library series as well as *The International Cooks' Catalogue* and *The Cooks' Catalogue*. She also writes and tests recipes.

Nan Mabon, a freelance food writer and cooking teacher in New York City, is also the cook for a private executive dining room on Wall Street. She studied at the Cordon Bleu in London.

Maurice Moore-Betty, owner-operator of The Civilized Art Cooking School, food consultant and restaurateur, is author of *Cooking for Occasions, The Maurice Moore-Betty Cooking School Book of Fine Cooking* and *The Civilized Art of Salad Making*.

Jane Moulton, a food writer for the *Plain Dealer* in Cleveland, took her degree in foods and nutrition. As well as reporting on culinary matters and reviewing food-related books for the *Plain Dealer,* she has worked in recipe development, public relations and catering.

Dorothy Parker, a freelance food writer, editor, and lecturer, is the author of *The Wonderful World of Yoghurt, Ms. Pinchpenny's Book of Kitchen Management*, and with Vera Gewanter, *Home Preserving Made Easy.*

Paul Rubinstein is the author of *Feasts for Two, The Night Before Cookbook* and *Feasts for Twelve (or More).* He is a stockbroker and the son of pianist Artur Rubinstein.

Maria Luisa Scott and Jack Denton Scott co-authored the popular *Complete Book of Pasta* and have also written many other books on food, including *Informal Dinners for Easy Entertaining, Mastering Microwave Cooking, The Best of the Pacific Cookbook*, and *Cook Like a Peasant, Eat Like a King*. With the renowned chef Antoine Gilly, they wrote *Feast of France.*

Satish Sehgal is the founder of the successful Indian Oven restaurant in New York City, which specializes in northern Indian cuisine. He began developing recipes for northern specialties while an engineering student in southern India and later abandoned engineering for the food world.

Kate Slate is a Senior Editor of the Great Cooks' Library series, as well as *The International Cooks' Catalogue* and *Where to Eat in America.*

Raymond Sokolov, author of *The Saucier's Apprentice*, is a freelance writer with a particular interest in food.

Paula Wolfert, author of *Mediterranean Cooking* and *Couscous and Other Good Food from Morocco*, is also a cooking teacher and consultant. She has written articles for *Vogue* and other magazines.

Nicola Zanghi is the owner-chef of Restaurant Zanghi in Glen Cove, New York. He started his apprenticeship under his father at the age of thirteen, and is a graduate of two culinary colleges. He has been an instructor at the Cordon Bleu school in New York City.

Contents

ICES AND GRANITES

FROZEN CAKES, PIES AND CONCOCTIONS

Ice Cream & Other Frozen Desserts

When we hear the phrase "frozen dessert," most 20th-century Americans immediately envision a fluted glass dish piled high with scoops of vanilla, chocolate or strawberry ice cream. The number of confections, however, that jostle one another under this rubric is enormous, encompassing ices, sherbets and *granite* and the latest passion of these fad-loving United States, frozen yogurt. Since the powers of imagination are limitless, so are the concoctions that combine ice cream or sherbet with other kinds of dessert foods; dreaming up new inventions has long been the favorite avocation of great cooks. From their warm kitchens come cool surprises —new frozen soufflés, frozen mousses, frozen cakes, pies and custards, in rich and fascinating profusion. The really innovative cook derives satisfaction from mixing—besides ingredients—food preparation methods; out of this creative urge have come countless frosty extravaganzas, such as the now classic fire-and-ice invention of Baked Alaska.

Before Edison. The concept of a frozen dessert—something delightful and contrasting in taste at the conclusion of a meal—is probably no more antique than the idea of freezing food, which may well date back to the Ice Age.

The earliest *formal* frozen dessert making occurred in Rome in the first century A.D., when Nero ordered an early Roman version of the bucket brigade to transport packed snow from the mountainsides to his groaning board, where it was then flavored with fruits, nuts and honey. Then, after a hiatus of a millenium or so, we know that Marco Polo introduced into Italy a product that had enchanted him in the Orient: a frozen dish that was probably the forerunner of what we know as milk ice—or sherbet. In the 16th century, flavored ices were imported—along with the table fork and other accoutrements of court life—to France from Italy by Catherine de Medici. And thence the notion spread to the British Isles and the rest of Europe.

Ice cream—at first dubbed "cream ice"—was apparently the invention of a French chef to Charles I of England, who tried to keep the recipe secret—about as successfully as he kept his throne. Once the exclusive indulgence of emperors and kings, by the end of the 17th century, ices, sherbets and ice cream were enjoyed by commoners as well, who flocked to elegant ice cream salons for these frozen treats.

At first introduction to American cuisine, ice cream was definitely a luxury item of European extraction and was enjoyed only by the privileged class. It was still a novelty in 1744 to the guest who described a strawberry ice cream (or ice cream with strawberries on it) that he was served by the Governor of Maryland. But it was soon to become the national dessert it remains today. George Washington evidently enjoyed it: At Mount Vernon, two pewter pots were reserved for ice cream making. Thomas Jefferson, who introduced Americans to many European foods, served the French innovation called *omelette surprise* (later to be renamed Baked Alaska) at state dinners.

Washington hostesses Mrs. Alexander Hamilton and Dolly Madison further popularized frozen desserts. At Madison's second inaugural ball, a dome of pink ice cream on a silver platter dominated the gala buffet.

As in Europe, this devotion to frozen dairy foods filtered down to the common man. To replace the tiresome and time-consuming task of beating the ice cream or sherbet in a metal bowl over ice and salt, a woman named Nancy Johnson originated the hand-cranked ice cream freezer—a boon to homemakers and entrepreneurs alike. Large-scale commercial production of ice cream began soon after. In the late 1800's, the ice cream soda was discovered when someone substituted ice cream for heavy cream in a popular drink made with fruit juices and carbonated water. This new ice cream soda was a hit at the Centennial celebrations in Philadelphia. Soda fountains became so popular that puritanically-minded citizens feared the loss of our moral strength and passed laws forbidding the sale of sodas on Sundays. Sometime between 1896 and 1900, however, an enterprising soda jerk got around the law by leaving out the carbonated water and calling his concoction a Sunday soda. Later, to dissociate this hardly less sinful delicacy from the Sabbath, the spelling was changed to sundae.

The Modern Ice Cream Industry. In this century, many innovations have transformed the making and serving of frozen desserts. According to legend, the birth of that great American institution, the ice cream cone, took place in St. Louis in 1904. A Syrian pastry salesman at the World's Fair of that year, so one version goes, was doing a land office business selling thin waffle-like crêpes when he noticed that an ice cream vendor at a nearby booth had run out of dishes for his wares. Whereupon, the waffle-maker started rolling up his product into cone shapes, which hardened to crisp as they were filled up by the ice cream seller.

In the 1920s, the Eskimo pie, the Good Humor bar and the popsicle were all invented in fairly rapid succession. And in 1939 the machine that makes soft ice cream was perfected. Today the U.S. ice cream industry is one of the country's largest and most profitable businesses.

Ice cream is made in more flavors than any other food you can think of. (Only race horses have been given more flamboyant and mystifying names.) Run through the several varieties offered daily by your local ice creamery—and then go on from there. Tanganilla, Pistachio Almond Fudge, Tutti-Fruitti, Mud, Pumpkin-Pie Marble, Brandied Apricot Almond, Danish Fruitcake, Pink Bubble Gum, Butternut Toffee, Apple Strudel, Root Beer, Rocky Road, Boysenberry Cheesecake, Peppermint Stick, Banana Marshmallow, Jolly Gingerbread, Green Tea, Shortberry Strawcake and Goody-

Goody Gumdrop are only some of the "flavors" that have come into being. Fortunately for us, some flavors such as Chile-con-Carne and Sauerkraut, didn't catch on and have passed into limbo. One of the leading U.S. manufacturers nonetheless has authenticated its invention of nearly 500 different flavors of ice cream so far—and the sky appears to be the limit.

We are also inundated with sherbets, ices, soft ice creams, ice cream sandwiches, cakes and bars, and, in some states, an imitation ice cream called mellorine, made with coconut oil instead of cream.

Some of these commercial preparations use high-quality ingredients, but others cut economic corners by substituting artificial flavorings and pumping the product up with air. Over a thousand chemical emulsifiers and stabilizers have legal sanction. The best way to know just what goes into the frozen desserts you eat is to make them at home. They will not only be free of chemical additives, they will be fresher, more nutritious and much better tasting. You will have control over the amount of butterfat and sweetening and can adapt them to fit your regimen and palate. Besides, with the possible exception of home-baked bread, there is nothing you can serve your family or guests that will impress them more than ice cream (or sherbet or ice) you've made yourself.

What's in a Name. As with any category so large and various as "frozen desserts," nomenclature can be confusing and usage is not always consistent.

Ice cream defines itself: Its basis is cream, the heavier the more delicious. It needs only the addition of a sweetening and a flavoring. Depending on the richness of the cream and the nature of the flavoring, its caloric value tends to be high.

French ice cream or frozen custard uses egg yolks and milk or cream heated together until the yolks thicken, instead of heavy cream alone. Occasionally flour or cornstarch is also used as a thickener. When it is made with cream it is richer than ice cream, higher both in calories and cholesterol. Since the egg yolks also act as an emulsifier, French ice cream has an especially smooth texture.

Ice milk is simply ice cream made with milk. It has less fat, fewer calories, and fewer milk solids. Most of the "softies" sold from vans or roadside stands are really soft ice milk, not ice cream.

Sherbet, a name which comes to us from the French *sorbet* (but ultimately goes back to the Arabic *sharbah*), is made from milk or cream, but proportionately less than in ice cream. Because the proportion of flavoring and sugar is greater than in ice cream or ice milk, sherbet may be only slightly lower in calories than ice cream. To distinguish them from ices, sherbets are sometimes called milk sherbets.

Ices have no milk at all. They are made from a sugar-syrup base to which flavorings and fruit purées may be added. Gelatin and stiffly beaten egg whites are sometimes used to stabilize ices and prevent the formation of large ice crystals. French *sorbet*, Italian *granita* and the coarse-textured, slushy drink called a *frappé* are all ices. Just to confuse matters, ices are sometimes called sherbets.

Frozen mousses are made in several different ways. One uses a custard base made of cooked egg yolks and sugar syrup (sometimes cornstarch or flour is added); another uses a meringue base of stiffly beaten egg whites and sugar syrup; another has only a sugar syrup base. Flavorings are added to the base and the mixture is folded into heavy whipped cream. Because mousses freeze well without churning (air having been already introduced into the cream and the eggs), they are often used to fill *bombes* and other molds.

Frozen soufflés are simply mousses frozen in a soufflé dish, usually with a paper or foil collar added so that the chilled sweet "rises" above the dish to give the illusion of a baked soufflé.

Parfait was once a coffee-flavored ice, but today it can refer to any ice cream layered with a sauce in a tall glass or to a mousse frozen in a mold.

Tortoni and spumone are Italian contributions to the spectrum of ice creams. *Biscuit tortoni*, invented by an Italian ice cream maker in 19th-century Paris, is a custard-based mousse flavored with sherry and topped with almonds. *Spumone* is a three-tiered *bombe*: a bottom layer of frozen custard, a filling of whipped and sweetened heavy cream and a top layer of custard-based mousse, each section having a different flavoring and color.

Making the Mix. The flavor and texture of ice creams, sherbets and ices depend on the ingredients and the methods used for freezing them. Cream and milk contribute to the smoothness and stability of frozen desserts. The richer the cream, the smoother the ice cream. Heavy cream must be 30 to 36 percent butterfat. It makes very smooth ice creams, and is essential for mousses. In making ice cream or sherbet, if you want to lower the cholesterol, use cream with a lower percentage of butterfat. Light cream is between 18 and 20 percent fat, while half-and-half contains only about 10 to 12 percent fat. Homogenized milk has even less; the minimum fat content required in most states is 3 percent. But if the butterfat is decreased, other ingredients may be needed to act as emulsifiers and stabilizers—that is, to keep the mixture from separating or forming large ice crystals during or after freezing. Egg yolks make good emulsifiers; they add cholesterol, but they also make a firmer and smoother frozen product. Ices and sherbets, which have little or no milk or cream in them, often depend on beaten egg whites, gelatin, cornstarch or corn syrup for their smoothness. Some fruits, such as currants and cranberries, have a lot of pectin, which acts as a natural stabilizer in frozen confections made with those fruits.

Sugar proportions should be heeded: Too much sugar will keep ice

Blender. A blender is not only handy for pureeing fresh fruits for sherbets, but is a marvelous aid in breaking up the large ice crystals that develop in still-frozen ice creams, sherbets and ices, making the end product much smoother.

cream, sherbet or ice from freezing properly. In sherbets and ices, the right proportion is one part sugar to four parts liquid, although many water ices which are served between courses of a meal have much less sugar. Alcohol also lowers the freezing point of the mixture; flavorings with alcohol in them should be used sparingly and added after the mixture is partially frozen. The anti-freeze qualities of alcohol, however, can be useful. If you are adding solid fruit, to keep it from freezing into hard little lumps, let it stand in some liquor for 3 or 4 hours before adding it to the ice cream mixture—brandy, rum, cognac, kirsch, sherry or vodka are good for this purpose. Fresh pineapple, which has an enzyme that wreaks havoc on proteins, must be cooked before it is added to ice cream; this is not necessary with canned pineapple or if preparing a water ice (without egg whites or gelatin).

When making ice cream, the basic mixture may be made well in advance of the freezing process; in fact, mixing the ingredients a day ahead will make a smoother texture and yield a greater volume of ice cream. It should at any rate always be chilled before freezing. Fruits, nuts, and other solids should only be added after the mixture is partially frozen. If you are using an ice cream freezer, put these ingredients in after the freezing process is complete and before packing the ice cream and leaving it to "ripen" in the freezer.

Freezer thermometer. To use freezer-model ice cream machines or to still-freeze ice cream, sherbet and ices successfully, it is essential that the freezer be cold enough—no higher than 5 F. A freezer thermometer will ensure success; the ideal temperature range, -10 to 5 F., is shaded on this model for easy reading.

Some terms connected with ice cream making that may seem arcane are "over-run," "ripening" and "tempering." Over-run refers to the increase in volume that occurs between the liquid and solid states. Many commercial ice creams double in volume in the freezing process; in home-made ice cream, the increase is only 25 to 30 percent. "Ripening" means mellowing finished ice cream by packing it down, insulating it and letting it stand at zero degrees for a while to harden. "Tempering" ice cream is keeping that hard-frozen product at room temperature for 10 or 15 minutes (or somewhat longer in the refrigerator) before serving it.

To freeze ice cream, sherbet or ices, there are several choices: A hand-cranked freezer, an electric freezer that uses ice and salt or an electric freezer that works inside the freezing compartment of a refrigerator or freezer. All three of these devices churn the mixture while it freezes, providing a smooth, even texture.

The mixture may also be still-frozen in ice trays or molds. Still-freezing is used for molded mousses and many sherbets and ices, although the latter two usually need to be beaten by hand or with an electric mixer at intervals as they harden. This method is less successful for ice cream.

Hand-Cranked Ice Cream Freezer. The best hand-cranked freezers

Ice cream freezer. An old-fashioned pine tub fitted with non-corrosive metal fixtures and wooden dashers (and filled with crushed ice and rock salt) will produce excellent ice cream. Available in sizes ranging from 2 to 20 quarts, this hand-cranked model is also available with an electric motor.

have a well-insulated outer bucket—usually of wood or fiberglass—to hold the layers of chipped ice and rock salt, and a metal container for the ice cream. The cranking mechanism, which attaches to the top of the bucket, causes either the dasher inside the canister or the container itself to revolve. As it turns, the dasher scrapes the ice cream mixture off the icy walls of the canister. One of its advantages over the model in which electricity does the work is that the speed of cranking can be regulated and hence will produce a smoother-textured ice cream. Another is that you can make a family (or community) project of ice cream making and share the labor in relays.

Fill the inner canister to no more than two-thirds its capacity, to allow for expansion. Position it in the bucket and start to add the ice. Fill the space between bucket and canister one-third full of ice. Then spread a handful of salt over it and alternate ice and salt until the bucket is almost full. Don't toss any salt on top of the canister unless you like salty ice cream. Most freezers require cracked ice, *not* ice cubes, and rock salt (coarse or kosher salt, *not* table salt). *Never use dry ice.* You will need about four parts ice to one part salt and it will take 25 pounds of ice to make a gallon of ice cream, or about four refrigerator trays of ice to make a quart. The larger the proportion of salt used, the faster the ice will melt and the more quickly the ice cream will freeze. But the ice cream should not freeze *too* quickly, since the churning makes it lighter and smoother. On the other hand, if it freezes too slowly, it will become buttery.

Having filled both canister and bucket, start cranking. At the beginning, about one revolution per second is best, then gradually speed up the motion. Like leaning downhill when learning to ski, it is against all natural impulses, since the cranking gets harder as you go along. But proceeding from slow to fast will reward you with a creamier ice cream. When the handle can hardly be turned any more, the ice cream is finished—after about 20 minutes of steady action.

The ice cream will still be soft and mushy. Remove the dasher and reward all crankers with a lick. Now is the time to stir in fruits, nuts, candy bits or other solids with a wooden spoon. Then, pack down the ice cream by plunging a wooden spoon several times into the mixture. Cover the canister, plug the hole with a cork, drain off the water that has accumulated in the bucket, add more ice and salt, insulate the bucket with an old blanket or quilt or lots of newspapers and let the ice cream ripen for several hours.

The ripening may also take place in a freezer. Transfer the ice cream from the canister to freezer containers and store it at 0 degrees for a few hours or overnight. Although it can be stored for up to a month, it will taste best the first week. To seal in flavors for a longer time, wrap the containers tightly with foil.

Electric Ice Cream Freezers. One type of electric freezer is built just like the hand-cranked machine, only an electric motor does the work. Fill the canister two-thirds full with the mixture to be frozen, and the bucket with layers of ice and salt, just as for a hand-operated freezer. Plug it in and listen to the sound of the motor; in about 20 minutes for ice cream, somewhat less for low-fat frozen yogurts, sherbets and ices, the motor will begin to labor. (Some models have a light to indicate when the mixture is done.) Turn the machine off and prepare the mixture for ripening as for hand-cranked ice cream, either in the bucket or in the freezer.

Another variety of electric machine, consisting of a metal canister, a plastic shell and a motor, requires no ice or salt. It works inside a deep-freeze or freezing compartment, and is left there for the 30 to 45 minutes it takes the dessert to reach a semi-frozen state. The machine does not need to be attended while it does the work; it automatically turns itself off when the mixture inside has reached the proper consistency. The mixture is then packed into freezer containers for the final hardening.

Frozen Yogurt. Yogurt is a newcomer in the frozen dessert game. In fact, yogurt in the *un*frozen state did not make its way to America until the 20th century, and did not really make it out of health food stores and into supermarkets until the 1960s. Now, however, we know what those centenarians in Georgia, U.S.S.R., have known for ages: that yogurt is good for you. The lactobacillus (bulgaricus and acidophilus) that converts milk into yogurt increases A and D vitamins, renders accessible the whole family of B vitamins and reduces cholesterol. It is a most beneficial food, to

Ice cream freezer and machine. Here are two modern, electric ice cream makers: The larger freezer uses ice cubes and table salt, and will make 2 quarts; the smaller model is placed right inside of a conventional freezer and will produce 1 quart of ice cream at a time.

Yogurt machines. The best frozen yogurt desserts are made with homemade yogurt. These machines perform that task by maintaining a steady level of heat, turning milk—plus yogurt starter—into yogurt. Both are equipped with 6-ounce glass jars and plastic lids in which to make and then store the yogurt.

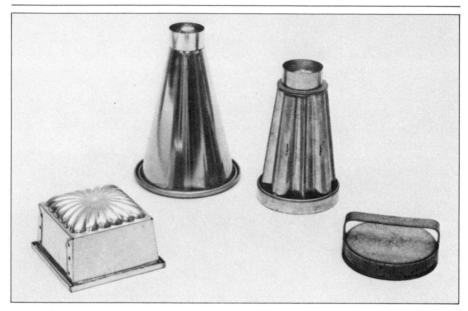

Square and cone-shaped ice cream molds. Mold plain ice cream or *bombes* into festive shapes in molds like these. Of heavy tinned or stainless steel, all are well constructed, with strong seams, rolled edges and tightly fitting lids. They are available in sizes ranging from approximately 1 cup to 1¾ quarts.

which almost magical powers of health promotion and healing have been attributed.

Magic or not, the homemade variety has advantages over the commercial, principal among them being that the nature and amount of substances added to it can be controlled. It also costs about one-half as much as commercial yogurt. Electric yogurt makers abound. They usually combine a low-heat unit with a group of 6- or 8-ounce covered containers. In such a contraption, milk—with a small amount of fresh yogurt culture stirred into it—will turn into yogurt in 5 to 10 hours. Any kind of milk can be used—whole or skim, homogenized or not, condensed or evaporated, pasteurized or raw. If using unpasteurized milk, bring it to a boil and then cool it to room temperature before adding the yogurt culture (too high heat will kill the yogurt bacteria).

Use the finished yogurt in any way you would use milk or cream to make a frozen dessert. Gelatin may be added for a finer texture. Ironically, in freezing yogurt the lactobacilli are killed, and some of yogurt's health-giving properties are lost. Relative to ice cream, however, it still wins the low-calorie and low-cholesterol prizes. As with other frozen desserts, it's best to let frozen yogurt thaw slightly before serving.

Spumone mold. Studded with candied fruits and nuts, the Italian specialty known as *spumone* should be frozen in a mold such as this one to be truly authentic. A seamless beehive of aluminum, equipped with a tight-fitting lid, the mold is available in both large or individual serving sizes.

Concoctions. Fancy frozen desserts, such as *bombes*, cakes, pies and crepes, are where the real fun comes in. They are not that much more difficult than making simple ice creams and ices; it's just that since they combine different foodstuffs and processes, they take more time. A *bombe* is a molded dessert, usually with a plain ice cream shell and a mousse filling. Ice cream cakes are made of layers of ice cream or sherbet and cake, sometimes in simple strata, sometimes rolled up like a jelly roll. Sponge cake works best for a cake roll. For easier handling, roll the cake in a towel as soon as it's baked and let it cool there. Then it will roll right up when put together with the ice cream. Or a hollowed-out cake may be filled with ice cream and frozen—an amusing way to combine ice cream and cake for a birthday party. Contrasting colors in cake and ice cream make for a pleasing effect. Let an ice cream cake defrost for 10 to 15 minutes before serving it; if it's refrozen, don't leave it in the freezer for more than 3 or 4 days.

Ice cream or frozen mousse makes an elegant filling for pie. Any type of pie crust may be used. A crumb crust—made of ground graham crackers, vanilla wafers or thin chocolate cookies—has an advantage, because it doesn't need baking first. But a pie shell made with a sweet dough and baked until lightly browned will also work. The main thing to remember is

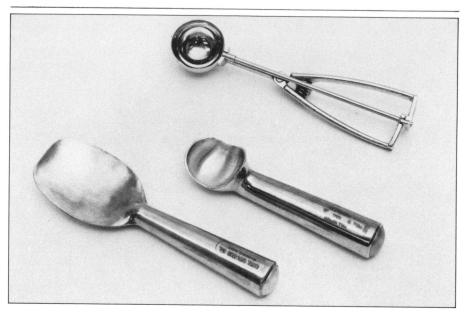

Ice cream spade and scoop and sherbet scoop. Filled with a special fluid that makes the metal warm relative to ice cream, this cast-aluminum spade (bottom) and scoop (middle) make quick work of solid-frozen ice cream. A sherbet scoop (top) works by means of a squeeze-action handle and comes in a large range of sizes.

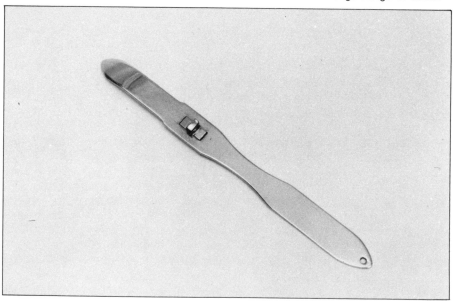

Citrus sheller. Lemon or orange shells to be stuffed with sherbet can be quickly prepared with this little gadget. It first lifts a strip of peel around the middle of the fruit, then gently pries the shells loose, leaving the fruit and shells intact. The fruit can then be used in the sherbet.

that it should be frozen for several hours before being filled. For the filling, avoid ices, sherbets or other frozen mixtures that break down quickly. A rich, full-bodied, smooth-textured custard ice cream or a mousse is best. Then it may be decorated with whipped cream shortly before serving.

Equipment. Aside from the ice cream freezers and yogurt makers already mentioned, the neophyte frozen dessert chef probably has in his general kitchen equipment almost everything he needs. An electric mixer and a blender will be useful for making the mix. Whisks for beating eggs and cream, a double boiler for preparing custard bases and melted chocolate, rubber scrapers and wooden spoons for moving soft-frozen sweets from freezing canister to freezer containers, will all come in handy. In addition, a refrigerator-freezer thermometer will allow you to make sure the climate of your refrigerator is no warmer than 45 F. and that the mercury hovers at 0 F. in the freezer. And because homemade ice cream is denser than commercial brands, it freezes harder, making a heavy-duty, professional scoop or spade for digging it out a real plus. Some scoops and spades come with a built-in defroster that softens the ice cream as they scoop. To graduate from basic training in ice cream cuisine, you may want to add an ice cream mold or two (they come in a variety of sizes and shapes) to your battery. Metal molds are recommended because they cool so quickly (and should always be chilled before working with them). And, if you are devoted to citrus ices and would like to serve them in the French style—ensconced in half shells or orange, grapefruit, lemon or tangerine —a citrus shell cutter will save precious minutes of preparation time—and tons of frustration.

Ice Cream

INDIAN ICE CREAM (KULFI)

Satish Sehgal

8 to 9 servings

Kulfi is an ancient Indian iced dish that has retained its popularity in spite of the advent of ice cream. It owes its delicious flavor to the large quantities of milk, almonds and pistachios used in its preparation. To freeze, the *kulfi* is conventionally placed in a number of small molds and immersed in crushed ice mixed with salt and niter (potassium nitrate). The vessel containing the ice and molds is then gently shaken with a rotary motion until the *kulfi* mixture freezes. The molds are of aluminum with tight-fitting screw caps.

6 CUPS MILK
2 TABLESPOONS CORNSTARCH, DIS-
   SOLVED IN A LITTLE COLD MILK
½ CUP SUGAR
¾ CUP POWDERED MILK
4 TABLESPOONS HEAVY CREAM
1 TABLESPOON SHREDDED, BLANCHED
   PISTACHIOS
1 TABLESPOON SHREDDED, BLANCHED
   ALMONDS
1 TABLESPOON ROSE WATER

1. Boil the milk for 5 minutes. Add the cornstarch and cook until the mixture thickens.

2. Add the sugar and stir until it dissolves.

3. Remove the pan from the heat. Add the powdered milk, heavy cream, pistachios and almonds. Let the mixture cook, then add the rose water.

4. When the mixture is at room temperature, divide it between 8 to 9 *kulfi* molds or other individual, ¾- to 1-cup ice cream molds, cover tightly, and freeze until three-quarters set. Remove the *kulfi* from the freezer, beat it with a fork and freeze again.

    Note: If you do not have individual molds, freeze the mixture in an ice tray.

5. Before serving, uncover each mold and roll it between the palms until the *kulfi* melts slightly. Then, hold it over a plate and give a sharp jerk to unmold the *kulfi*.

Note: Although *kulfi* freezes harder than ordinary ice cream, it melts at a comparatively faster rate, and should be eaten immediately after unmolding.

FRENCH VANILLA ICE CREAM

Linda Lewis

2½ quarts

History tells us that ice cream was perfected by French chefs in the 16th Century. Since this is a perfect recipe, logically it must be French. I like to think of it as French for another reason, too, for this ice cream makes a new and tasty use of dried out, end-of-the-line vanilla beans, and the French are nothing if not frugal and inventive with every scrap that passes through the kitchen. I use vanilla beans to make my own vanilla sugar for baking, and after several months in the sugar canister, they dry out and need to be replaced. I can't stand to see things go to waste any more than the French can (especially anything so expensive as vanilla beans), so I save the dried beans and after I have accumulated several, grind them to a fine powder in a small coffee or spice mill. I developed this velvety rich ice cream, flecked with specks of vanilla, as one way of putting that powder to good use.

4 EGGS, LIGHTLY BEATEN
1½ CUPS SUGAR
½ TEASPOON SALT
2 CUPS MILK
2 CUPS LIGHT CREAM
1 TABLESPOON VANILLA POWDER*
4 CUPS COLD HEAVY CREAM

1. In the top of a double boiler, combine the eggs, sugar and salt. Whisk in the milk and the light cream and cook over simmering water, stirring constantly, until the mixture thickens slightly. Remove from the heat.

2. Add the vanilla powder, straining it through a fine-meshed sieve to remove any large pieces. Stir thoroughly to prevent any vanilla particles from massing together. Refrigerate for several hours or overnight.

3. Remove the cold custard from the refrigerator and blend in the cold heavy cream.

4. Pour the mixture into the container of an ice cream maker and freeze according to the manufacturer's instructions.

*To make vanilla powder, grind several dried vanilla beans in a spice mill (a thoroughly cleaned coffee grinder will also work); one 4" bean will yield just a touch over 2 teaspoons of powder. The powder can then be stored for months in a tightly closed jar and can be used, measure for measure, in any dessert calling for vanilla extract. Just remember that the tiny vanilla specks will show. If you do not have dried vanilla beans on hand buy fresh beans and leave them in a warm dry place (like a pilot-lit oven) to dry out.

BISCUIT TORTONI LOAF

Florence Fabricant

12 servings

6 TABLESPOONS CRUSHED *AMARETTI*
  COOKIES (ITALIAN MACAROONS)
1¼ CUPS SUGAR
6 TABLESPOONS WATER
½ CUP SLICED ALMONDS
½ RAW POTATO
3 EGG WHITES
4 TABLESPOONS LIGHT RUM
2 CUPS HEAVY CREAM

1. Oil a 6-cup, square or rectangular loaf pan or ice cream mold. Line the bottom and two opposite sides with a single, long sheet of waxed paper, placing it across the mold so that the ends of the paper extend beyond the rim of the mold. Oil the paper.

   Note: A straight-sided, rather than a fancy, fluted mold will be easier to unmold.

2. Dust the inside of the mold with half of the *amaretti* crumbs, evenly spreading those that do not adhere to the sides over the bottom. Refrigerate the mold and turn your freezer to a very cold setting.

3. In a shallow pan, dissolve ½ cup of the sugar and 2 tablespoons of water and cook over medium heat without stirring.

4. Meanwhile, oil a marble slab or a large sheet of foil.

5. When the sugar mixture has turned a golden, honey-brown, add the almonds and stir briefly.

6. Pour the mixture onto the marble or foil and immediately spread the almond caramel until thin and even with the flat cut surface of the potato. Allow to cool.

7. Dissolve the remaining ¾ cup of sugar in ¼ cup of water and cook to the soft ball stage, 237 F. to 239 F. on a candy thermometer.

8. While the sugar is cooking, beat the egg whites until they form soft peaks. Gradually pour the hot sugar syrup into the egg whites, beating constantly. Continue beating for about 5 minutes, until stiff and glossy.

9. Add the rum, a tablespoon at a time, beating the egg whites for 30 seconds after each addition. Refrigerate the meringue.

10. Beat the cream until stiff; refrigerate.

11. Chop the hardened almond praline until uniformly minced, not finely ground. This is best done by hand rather than in a blender or food processor.

12. Combine the chopped caramel with the remaining *amaretti* crumbs.

13. Fold the whipped cream into the meringue and spoon half of it into the prepared mold. Cover with all but 2 tablespoons of the praline-*amaretti* mixture. Spoon in the rest of the meringue mixture and sprinkle the top with the reserved crumbs.

14. Cover with waxed paper and freeze for 24 hours, or longer.

15. To unmold, run a knife along the sides of the mold, being careful to stay between the waxed paper and the mold. Invert on a serving platter, lift off the mold and peel off

the paper.

16. Serve at once. The *tortoni* need not be decorated, although fresh raspberries or peaches poached in white wine do go well with it.

FRESH RASPBERRY ICE CREAM WITH FRAMBOISE

Ruth Ellen Church

About 1 gallon

For years I've made a basic ice cream with sundry variations, and try to have a new one every year for summer visitors at the family farm. The family and guests have nothing but joyous comments about this one. Pure fruit brandy, not the liqueur, is needed for best flavor.

2 CUPS SUGAR
¼ CUP CORNSTARCH
¼ TEASPOON SALT
1 QUART EACH OF MILK AND HEAVY
   CREAM OR 2 QUARTS HALF-AND-HALF
4 EGGS, BEATEN
2 PINTS FRESH RASPBERRIES, OR
2 PACKAGES FROZEN RASPBERRIES,
   CRUSHED, AND SIEVED TO REMOVE
   SEEDS
1 TABLESPOON VANILLA
½ CUP *FRAMBOISE*

1. In a 2-quart saucepan, combine the sugar, cornstarch and salt.

2. Add half the milk and cream (or half-and-half) gradually and cook and stir over moderate heat until thickened.

3. Whisk a little of the hot cream mixture into the beaten eggs, then add the warmed eggs to the rest of the cream mixture, and cook, stirring, about 2 minutes more.

4. Remove from the heat and add the raspberries, vanilla and *framboise*.

5. Chill, then turn into a freezer can and add the remaining milk and cream. Mix with a long-handled spoon or a few turns of the dasher.

6. Freeze according to the manufacturer's directions.

7. Transfer the ice cream to a plastic container, cover and place in the freezer to become firm.

Note: I've found that where I can't get rock salt for my freezer, canning salt or table salt will work—although not quite as efficiently.

CAPPUCCINO ICE CREAM

Nicola Zanghi

1 ½ quarts

1 ½ CUPS STRONG *ESPRESSO*, COOLED
4 TABLESPOONS INSTANT COFFEE
2 TABLESPOONS DARK RUM
1 ¼ CUPS SUGAR
1 TEASPOON GROUND CINNAMON
2 CUPS HEAVY CREAM

1. In a bowl, blend together the *espresso*, instant coffee, rum, sugar and cinnamon until the sugar dissolves.

2. Add the cream, mix well and place in the container of an ice cream maker.

3. Freeze according to the manufacturer's instructions. Remove from the ice cream maker and place in the freezer for several hours.

4. Serve with wafer-type cookies or garnish with chocolate curls.

Note: To make this without an ice cream freezer, first beat the cream until stiff, then follow Step 1. Stir the coffee mixture into the whipped cream, beat over salted ice until thick, and place in the freezer, stirring occasionally.

BROWN BREAD ICE CREAM

Maurice Moore-Betty

6 to 8 servings

Brown bread ice cream is an Edwardian specialty, a very English dessert. It has been served for years at Gunters Restaurant in London.

6 OUNCES (ABOUT 7 SLICES, TRIMMED)
  FRESH WHOLE-GRAIN BREAD CRUMBS
2 CUPS HEAVY CREAM
6 OUNCES (ABOUT ¾ CUP) VANILLA
  SUGAR (AVAILABLE IN SPECIALTY
  FOOD SHOPS)
2 OUNCES (ABOUT ¼ CUP) GRANULATED
  SUGAR
¼ CUP WATER
2 EGG WHITES
DARK CHOCOLATE*, MELTED
  (OPTIONAL)

1. Dry the bread crumbs in the oven until lightly browned and crisp.

2. Beat the cream until stiff, adding the vanilla sugar gradually.

3. In a saucepan, simmer the granulated sugar and water together for 2 to 3 minutes. Allow to cool.

4. Stir the bread crumbs into the sugar syrup and fold the mixture into the beaten cream.

5. Beat the egg whites until they hold peaks. Fold them gently into the cream and crumb mixture.

   Note: Do not beat the egg whites until you need them. Beaten too soon, they weep and become deflated.

6. Turn into cake pans or a pan lined with melted dark chocolate, if desired, and freeze.

7. Unmold onto a cold dish and serve in small slices.

*Use bitter or semisweet according to taste.

GEORGIA PEACH ICE CREAM

Nan Mabon

12 or more servings

We had a peach tree in our front yard in Atlanta and one of the great family rituals of the summer was the making of peach ice cream in an old hand-cranked ice cream freezer. This is the old family formula.

8 MEDIUM-SIZED PEACHES
3 CUPS HALF-AND-HALF
½ CUP WHIPPING CREAM
1 VANILLA BEAN OR 1 TEASPOON
  VANILLA EXTRACT
1⅓ CUPS SUGAR*
4 EGG YOLKS

1. Peel and pit the peaches. Purée coarsely in a blender or food processor; there should still be tiny chunks. Set aside.

2. In a heavy, enameled pan, heat the half-and-half, cream and the vanilla bean (if using a vanilla extract, do not add until later).

3. In a mixing bowl, combine the sugar and egg yolks, and slowly pour on half of the hot cream, whisking constantly. Remove the vanilla bean.

4. Return the cream-egg mixture to the pan with the remaining cream and cook slowly, stirring constantly. Stir with the spoon into the corners and all over the bottom of the pan. When the mixture becomes custardy in consistency (it should be thick enough to coat the back of a spoon), remove from the heat. Let it cool and then remove the vanilla bean. If using vanilla extract, stir it in when the mixture is cool.

5. Pour the cooled custard mixture into the container of an ice cream maker and freeze according to the manufacturer's instructions.

Note: If using a hand-cranked ice cream maker, I find that it helps to make the custard in advance and completely chill it in the refrigerator before putting it in the freezer.
*If the peaches are very sweet, use only 1¼ cups sugar.

19

CINNAMON ICE CREAM

Maurice Moore-Betty

6 to 8 servings

This is an English ice cream that was popular at the turn of the century. I think it is an acquired taste!

2 CUPS HEAVY CREAM
½ CUP SUGAR
2 TABLESPOONS GROUND CINNAMON
4 EGG YOLKS
1 CUP MILK

1. In the top half of a double boiler, heat the cream, sugar and cinnamon over gentle heat.

2. Beat the egg yolks and milk together, blending thoroughly.

3. Add the egg-milk mixture to the cream mixture. Cook slowly, stirring constantly, until thickened. Do not let it boil or it will curdle.

4. Chill and freeze in an ice cream freezer or machine, according to the manufacturer's instructions.

Note: Homemade ice creams are better eaten soon after they have been made. Anyway, they're so good they don't last long.

CARAMEL ICE CREAM

Satish Sehgal

8 servings

This ice cream came to India by way of the British and the French, and the Indian upper class adopted it swiftly. I learned the recipe from the chef at my restaurant, who once worked for a British Army major.

6 CUPS MILK
2 EGGS, SEPARATED
½ CUP SUGAR
2 TABLESPOONS BOILING WATER
2 TABLESPOONS BUTTER
1 TEASPOON UNFLAVORED GELATIN,
    DISSOLVED IN 1 TABLESPOON BOILING
    WATER
1 CUP HEAVY CREAM, WHIPPED

1. Scald 3 cups of milk.

2. Beat the egg yolks and ¼ cup of the sugar until lemon in color.

3. Into the top half of a double boiler, pour the egg yolk mixture and scalded milk and

cook, slowly, until the mixture coats the back of a spoon. Set aside to cool.

4. In a small saucepan, heat the remaining ¼ cup sugar with 2 tablespoons of hot water until it turns a rich, golden brown color.

5. Add the remaining 3 cups of milk and simmer until the caramel is completely dissolved. Remove from the heat and add the butter and gelatin.

6. Turn this mixture into the cooled custard.

7. Beat the egg whites until stiff, then fold them into the caramel custard mixture.

8. Pour into a shallow pan or tray and place in the freezer until it is three-quarters set, about 35 to 45 minutes. Remove from the freezer, beat with a fork and fold in the whipped cream. Freeze again until set.

SPUMONE DI TAORMINA

Nicola Zanghi

6 to 8 servings

This is the real McCoy—not your paper-lined wedge studded with tutti-frutti, but the real Sicilian specialty accented with the flavor of blood oranges.

VEGETABLE OIL
GRATED RIND OF 1 BLOOD ORANGE*
¼ CUP FINELY CHOPPED TOASTED
  ALMONDS
¼ CUP FINELY CHOPPED CANDIED FRUIT
3 TABLESPOONS ORANGE LIQUEUR
¼ TEASPOON VANILLA EXTRACT

1 PINT HEAVY CREAM, BEATEN UNTIL
  STIFF
¾ CUP SUGAR
4 TABLESPOONS LIGHT CORN SYRUP
6 EGGS AT ROOM TEMPERATURE,
  WELL BEATEN

1. Brush a 6-cup spumone (or other ice cream) mold with the vegetable oil.

2. Fold the rind, almonds, candied fruit, liqueur and vanilla into the whipped cream. Place in the refrigerator.

3. In a saucepan, combine the sugar and corn syrup and cook to 220 F. on a candy thermometer (just below the soft ball stage.)

4. Pour this syrup slowly into the eggs, whisking constantly. When all of the syrup has been incorporated, beat the mixture over ice until cool.

5. Fold the egg mixture into the chilled whipped cream and turn into the mold. Freeze overnight.

6. Unmold the spumone by dipping it in tepid or lukewarm water. Be very careful not to use water any hotter than tepid, as this will cause the ingredients to separate.

*Blood oranges are not easy to come by in this country, so to strike the proper note of authenticity, substitute a regular orange and use several drops of red food coloring. Or, for an interesting twist, substitute grated tangerine rind.

CREAMY CHOCOLATE ICE CREAM

Linda Lewis

2 quarts

I developed this recipe to meet the demands of a chocolate crazy family. A rich chocolate custard and the beaten egg whites into which it is folded are the basic ingredients in this exquisite chocolate ice cream.

1 CUP MILK
6 OUNCES (1 CUP) SEMISWEET
  CHOCOLATE BITS
3 EGGS, SEPARATED
1 CUP SUPERFINE SUGAR
1 TABLESPOON VANILLA EXTRACT
⅛ TEASPOON SALT
2 CUPS LIGHT CREAM
1 CUP HEAVY CREAM

1. In the top of a double boiler, combine the milk and the chocolate bits over simmering water. Stir occasionally with a wooden spoon until the mixture is thoroughly blended and the milk has scalded.

2. Meanwhile, beat the egg yolks lightly in a small mixing bowl. Add ½ cup of the sugar and beat until thick.

3. Gradually beat in several tablespoons of the hot chocolate milk to warm the beaten egg yolk mixture. Pour the warmed egg yolk mixture in a thin stream into the chocolate milk in the double boiler, stirring constantly. Continue stirring over simmering water until the custard is thick enough to coat the spoon.

4. Stir in the vanilla, remove from the heat and cool.

5. Beat the egg whites with the salt until frothy. Gradually add the remaining ½ cup sugar, a few tablespoons at a time, and beat until thick and glossy.

6. Using a rubber spatula, fold the cooled chocolate custard into the beaten egg whites; blend in the light and heavy cream.

7. Pour into the canister of an ice cream machine and freeze according to the manufacturer's instructions.

VANILLA AND CHERRY ICE CREAM BALLS

Bianca Brown

12 servings

1 JAR (17 OUNCES DARK, SWEET, PITTED
  CHERRIES IN HEAVY SYRUP
3 TABLESPOONS DARK RUM OR *KIRSCH*
1 QUART VANILLA ICE CREAM
1½ CUPS FINELY CHOPPED TOASTED
  ALMONDS

1. Put a jelly-roll pan—or enough cake tins to hold twelve 3"-diameter ice cream balls—into the freezer to chill.

2. Drain the syrup from the cherries into a small saucepan. Boil the syrup until it is reduced to ½ cup.

3. Stir in the rum or *kirsch,* then pour the syrup over the cherries. Cover and let them stand at room temperature for 24 hours.

4. Fill an ice cream scoop 2⅝" in diameter half full of the vanilla ice cream.

5. Leave the ice cream in the scoop and with the back of a small spoon, make an indentation in the center. Put 2 cherries in the indentation, cover them with more ice cream and unmold the ball onto the chilled jelly-roll pan.

6. Repeat, making 11 more ice cream balls.

7. Freeze them for 1 hour, or until the ice cream has hardened. Then, sprinkle the balls all over with the chopped nuts, pressing them into the ice cream, and return them to the freezer.

Note: Use the remaining cherries in a fruit salad.

ORANGE BLOSSOM ICE CREAM

Mireille Johnston

6 servings

3 CUPS MILK
7 EGG YOLKS, BEATEN
⅓ CUP SUGAR, APPROXIMATELY
2 TABLESPOONS ORANGE BLOSSOM
   WATER, APPROXIMATELY
½ TABLESPOON VANILLA EXTRACT
1 OUNCE DARK, UNSWEETENED
   CHOCOLATE
MINT LEAVES

1. Scald the milk.

2. In a heavy saucepan, beat the egg yolks and sugar until very thick and lemon colored. Stirring constantly, slowly pour in the hot milk.

3. Place over moderately low heat and stir constantly with a wooden spoon. Let the custard cool at room temperature, then chill in the refrigerator.

4. Stir the orange blossom water and vanilla into the chilled custard. Taste to see if the mixture is sweet enough and flavored enough (freezing mutes the taste, so it should be fairly strong), and correct if necessary. Place the mixture in an ice cream freezer and turn until smooth and thick.

5. Pack into a mold, cover with foil and place in the freezer for several hours or overnight.

6. Put the piece of chocolate on a sheet of waxed paper on the top of the stove near the

Continued from preceding page

pilot light or in a low oven. When it has softened somewhat, shave off little curls of chocolate with a potato peeler or a sharp knife.

7. Decorate a large platter with mint leaves. Run the mold quickly under hot water and invert the ice cream onto the platter. Sprinkle the chocolate curls on top and serve.

FRENCH QUARTER PRALINE ICE CREAM

Linda Lewis

2 quarts

Pecan Praline:
VEGETABLE SHORTENING
⅔ CUP SUGAR
6 TABLESPOONS WATER
1 CUP TOASTED PECANS (SMALL
   HALVES OR LARGE PIECES)

¾ CUP SUPERFINE SUGAR
¼ CUP LIGHT CORN SYRUP
2 EGGS, SEPARATED
1 TABLESPOON VANILLA EXTRACT
⅛ TEASPOON SALT
1 CUP HEAVY CREAM

Other Ingredients:
2 CUPS MILK

1. Oil a jelly-roll pan or a marble slab with flavorless vegetable shortening.

2. In a saucepan, combine the sugar and 6 tablespoons of water over medium-high heat and bring to a boil.

3. Cook until the syrup turns a golden brown color (about 4 to 5 minutes), then stir in the toasted pecans.

4. Bring the syrup back to a boil, then remove from the heat and pour onto the oiled surface.

5. Using two buttered forks, separate the pecan pieces and allow to cool.

6. In the top of a double boiler, scald the milk over rapidly boiling water. Reduce to a simmer and stir in ½ cup of the sugar and the corn syrup.

7. In a small mixing bowl, beat the egg yolks lightly with a fork. Gradually beat in about 6 tablespoons (about ⅓ cup) of the hot milk to warm the yolks.

8. Pour the warm egg yolk mixture in a thin stream into the milk remaining in the double boiler, stirring constantly with a wooden spoon. Continue stirring over simmering water until the custard is thick enough to coat the spoon.

9. Stir in the vanilla. Remove from the heat and cool.

10. Using a hand or electric mixer, beat the egg whites with the salt until frothy. Gradually add the remaining ¼ cup of sugar, a tablespoon at a time, beating until stiff and glossy.

11. Fold the egg whites into the cooled custard, then fold in the heavy cream.

12. Pour into the container of an ice cream maker and begin to freeze according to the

manufacturer's instructions.

13. When the ice cream is partially frozen and mushy in consistency, stir in the pecan praline and continue to freeze until firm.

FOUR FRUIT ICE CREAM

Jane Moulton

25 servings

2 CUPS SUGAR
3 ENVELOPES UNFLAVORED GELATIN
2½ CUPS LIGHT CREAM OR MILK
2 CANS (13 OUNCES EACH) EVAPORATED MILK OR EVAPORATED SKIM MILK (*NOT* SWEETENED CONDENSED)
3 MEDIUM-SIZED BLACK-RIPE BANANAS, PEELED

1 CAN (6 OUNCES) FROZEN LEMONADE CONCENTRATE, PARTIALLY THAWED
1 CAN (6 OUNCES) FROZEN PINEAPPLE JUICE CONCENTRATE, PARTIALLY THAWED
1 CAN (6 OUNCES) FROZEN ORANGE JUICE CONCENTRATE, PARTIALLY THAWED
1 TABLESPOON VANILLA EXTRACT

1. In a 4-quart saucepan, combine the sugar and gelatin. Gradually stir in the light cream or milk. Stir over medium heat until the sugar and gelatin dissolve.

2. Remove from the heat and stir in the evaporated milk.

3. Place the bananas, lemonade, pineapple juice and orange juice concentrates and vanilla in a blender container. Blend until smooth.

4. Add the fruit mixture to the cream-milk mixture and mix well; chill.

5. Freeze in an ice cream freezer according to the manufacturer's instructions. To freeze without an ice cream machine, freeze in a metal bowl until the edges are solid. Beat well with a rotary or electric mixer. Freeze again until almost solid and beat again. Cover and freeze solid.

Note: If a 1-quart, electric ice cream freezer is to be used, this recipe will have to be frozen in three batches. It is inconvenient to cut down the recipe because of the size of the cans.

Frozen Yogurt

APRICOT-PECAN FROZEN YOGURT

Kate Slate

1 quart

If you are making your own yogurt base (highly recommended), you must start this recipe at least 17 hours before you plan to serve the dessert. If you decide to make the dessert at the last minute, make sure the commercial yogurt you use is made with whole milk. Natural whole-milk yogurts from California are best; but a good low-fat yogurt will do if you add ½ cup of heavy cream for every 4 cups of yogurt.

Yogurt Base*:
2 TABLESPOONS BOILING WATER
1½ TEASPOONS UNFLAVORED GELATIN
3 CUPS MILK
1 CUP LIGHT CREAM
1 TABLESPOON HONEY
2 TEASPOONS PLAIN YOGURT (ANY
  NATURAL COMMERCIAL BRAND
  WILL DO)

Other Ingredients:
⅓ CUP APRICOT CONCENTRATE
  (AVAILABLE AT HEALTH FOOD
  STORES)
¼ CUP HONEY
½ CUP CHOPPED DRIED APRICOTS
½ CUP CHOPPED PECANS

1. In a small bowl, add the boiling water to the gelatin; stir until dissolved and set aside.

2. Place the milk, cream and honey in a saucepan and slowly bring to a boil. Just as it comes to a boil, remove the pan from the heat. Add the gelatin and set the pan aside to cool.

3. When the temperature of the milk drops to 110 F. (use a candy or dairy thermometer), pour off ¼ cup and put it in a small bowl.

4. Add the plain yogurt to the ¼ cup milk and whisk until completely homogenized. Return the milk-yogurt mixture to the rest of the milk and blend together.

5. Place the yogurt base in an electric yogurt maker for the amount of time specified in the manufacturer's instructions.

6. When the yogurt is done, refrigerate it for 4 hours or more.

   Note: It is best to make the evening before you plan to serve the dessert: Leave the yogurt in the yogurt maker overnight. Then, take it out and refrigerate it the next morning. It will be ready for freezing that afternoon.

7. Empty the chilled yogurt base into a mixing bowl and add the apricot concentrate, honey and apricots. Blend well.

   Note: Don't be alarmed if the butter fat in the yogurt base has risen to the top and congealed. It will be incorporated into the yogurt during the freezing process.

8. Refrigerate for 1 hour (2 hours if the apricots are very dry).

9. Add the pecans to the yogurt base just before pouring it into an ice cream freezer.

10. Freeze according to the manufacturer's instructions.

*If you prefer, you may substitute 1 quart of commercial yogurt for the yogurt base.

FROZEN YOGURT SUPREME

Dorothy Parker

4 to 6 servings

2 TABLESPOONS WATER
1 ENVELOPE UNFLAVORED GELATIN
1⅔ CUPS PLAIN YOGURT
⅓ CUP HEAVY CREAM
1 TABLESPOON HONEY
1 TABLESPOON BRANDY OR COGNAC
¼ CUP CHOPPED WALNUT MEATS
½ CUP PITTED AND CHOPPED RIPE RED
    CHERRIES
½ CUP PITTED AND CHOPPED DATES

1. In the top of a double boiler over low heat, put the 2 tablespoons of water. Sprinkle on the gelatin and leave on the burner for a few minutes.

2. When the gelatin has softened, remove it from the heat and stir in the yogurt, cream and honey. Transfer the mixture to an ice cube tray and put it into the freezer until semi-frozen.

3. Spoon the brandy or cognac over the nuts, cherries and dates and let them soak for 30 minutes.

4. When the yogurt mixture has half-frozen, remove it from the freezer, stir in the fruit-nut mixture, distributing it evenly. Put the yogurt back into the freezer and leave it for 3 to 4 hours.

5. Remove the supreme from the freezer and let it thaw for 10 minutes or so before serving.

FROZEN GINGER-PEACH YOGURT

Elizabeth Schneider Colchie

About 1 quart

¾ POUND (ABOUT 3 MEDIUM-SIZED) RIPE
   PEACHES, UNPEELED, PITTED AND
   COARSELY CHOPPED
⅓ CUP PALE HONEY
1 TABLESPOON LEMON JUICE
2 TABLESPOONS VERY FINELY MINCED
   PRESERVED GINGER IN SYRUP, PLUS
   2 TABLESPOONS OF THE SYRUP

1 EGG, SEPARATED
⅛ TEASPOON SALT
⅛ TEASPOON CREAM OF TARTAR
2 TABLESPOONS SUPERFINE SUGAR
2 CUPS WHOLE-MILK YOGURT

1. In a saucepan, combine the peaches, honey, lemon juice, ginger and ginger syrup and bring to a boil. Boil gently, stirring often, for 10 minutes, or until the fruit is soft.

2. In a medium-sized bowl, beat the egg yolk a moment; then add the hot peach mixture a little at a time, stirring vigorously.

3. In a small bowl, beat the egg white with the salt and cream of tartar until soft peaks form; beat in the superfine sugar, ½ tablespoon at a time, beating until stiff peaks form.

4. Stir the yogurt into the fruit mixture; then fold in the egg white.

5. Turn the mixture into a 1-quart ice cream freezer and follow the manufacturer's instructions for freezing.

LEMONY BANANA FROZEN YOGURT

Kate Slate

1 quart

2 VERY RIPE BANANAS
½ CUP LOOSELY-PACKED DARK BROWN
   SUGAR
1 RECIPE YOGURT BASE (PAGE 26), OR
   1 QUART COMMERCIAL, WHOLE-MILK
   YOGURT
1 TABLESPOON GRATED LEMON ZEST
1 JUST-RIPE BANANA

1. In a blender or food processor, combine the very ripe bananas and the brown sugar and purée.

2. Add the banana purée and lemon zest to the yogurt.

3. Cut the just-ripe banana into quarters lengthwise and then into ¼''-thick slices. Add the slices to the yogurt mixture.

4. Refrigerate for 1 hour, then freeze in an ice cream freezer according to the manufacturer's instructions.

CALIFORNIA YOGURT DESSERT

Kate Slate

1 quart

1 RECIPE YOGURT BASE (PAGE 26), OR
  1 QUART COMMERCIAL, WHOLE MILK
  YOGURT
½ CUP LOOSELY-PACKED LIGHT BROWN
  SUGAR
¼ TEASPOON ALMOND EXTRACT
⅔ CUP DRIED CURRANTS
¼ CUP WHITE SESAME SEEDS, TOASTED
¼ CUP SUNFLOWER SEEDS

1. Place the yogurt in a large bowl; sprinkle the brown sugar evenly over the top and mix in.

2. Add the almond extract and currants, and blend.

3. Refrigerate for 1 hour (2 hours if the currants are very dry).

4. Add the sesame and sunflower seeds to the yogurt mixture just before pouring it into the ice cream freezer.

5. Freeze according to the manufacturer's instructions.

FROZEN ORANGE YOGURT

Jane Moulton

1 quart

¾ CUP SUGAR
1 ENVELOPE UNFLAVORED GELATIN
1 CUP WHIPPING CREAM
1 CAN (6 OUNCES) FROZEN ORANGE
  JUICE CONCENTRATE, SLIGHTLY
  THAWED
2 CUPS PLAIN YOGURT
1 TEASPOON ORANGE EXTRACT
1 TEASPOON VANILLA EXTRACT

1. In a medium-sized saucepan, combine the sugar and gelatin. Add the whipping cream and stir over medium heat until the sugar and gelatin dissolve.

2. Remove from the heat and stir in the orange juice concentrate.

3. Using a wire whisk or the blender, beat in the yogurt, orange and vanilla extracts.

4. Place in an ice cream freezer and freeze according to the manufacturer's instructions. To freeze without an ice cream freezer, pour the mixture into a flat-bottomed metal pan and place in the freezer. When the edges are frozen, remove to a mixing bowl and beat well. Return to the freezer. Beat again when almost solid. When frozen, place in a deeper container with a lid.

Sherbet

BRANDIED APRICOT SHERBET

Florence Fabricant

1½ quarts

1 CUP DRIED APRICOTS
1 CUP SUGAR
2 CUPS FRESH ORANGE JUICE
2 TABLESPOONS COGNAC
2 EGG WHITES

1. In a heavy saucepan, combine the apricots and 1½ cups of water. Simmer, uncovered, until the apricots are very soft and most of the water has evaporated, about 20 minutes. Watch carefully so they do not scorch.

2. Force the apricots through a sieve to purée them.

3. Boil the sugar with another 1½ cups of water for about 8 minutes, or until a candy thermometer registers 215 F. to 218 F., just under the jelly stage. Mix this sugar syrup with the apricot purée.

4. Add the orange juice and cognac to the purée.

5. Pour the mixture into a bread pan or freezer tray with a capacity of at least 6 cups and freeze for 1 hour or longer, until the mixture has begun to harden around the edges but is still mushy in the center. Stir the mixture thoroughly.

6. Return to the freezer and freeze until fairly firm, stirring every 40 minutes or so. The more you stir, the better the texture will be.

7. When the sherbet is firm but not solid, beat the egg whites until stiff, but not dry. Fold them carefully but thoroughly into the sherbet. Freeze at least 1 hour longer before serving.

    Note: The finished sherbet may be transferred to a plastic container for more convenient storage.

8. Place the sherbet in the refrigerator for 20 minutes before serving to allow it to soften a little.

Note: To make the sherbet in an electric ice cream maker, complete Steps 1 through 4 and chill the mixture for 1 hour. Then fold in the egg whites and freeze according to the manufacturer's directions. If the ice cream freezer has a capacity of only 1 quart, reduce the quantities to ⅔ cup apricots, 2 cups water, ⅔ cup sugar, 1⅓ cups orange juice, 4 teaspoons cognac and 1 egg white.

PEAR SHERBET

Susan Lipke

1 quart

The success of this essence-of-pear sherbet depends upon the observation of two rules. First, the pears must be firm-ripe and unblemished; and, once you start, you must proceed quickly through the recipe. All the ingredients should be measured and all equipment at the ready before you start. The reason for these cautions is that if you dawdle, or if the pears are overripe, the sherbet mixture will turn an unappetizing brown before it freezes. If properly prepared, it stays very pale.

3 LEMONS
2 POUNDS (ABOUT 4 LARGE) FIRM-RIPE,
  UNBLEMISHED PEARS
¾ CUP SUGAR
1 TO 2 TABLESPOONS *POIRE WILLIAMS*
  (PEAR *EAU-DE-VIE*)

1. Squeeze the lemons, measure out ⅓ cup of the juice and set aside. In a medium-sized mixing bowl, combine the rest of the lemon juice with about 1 quart of water.

2. Quickly peel, halve and core the pears, dropping them immediately into the acidulated water.

3. Remove only as many pear halves as can be puréed at one time from the water and place them in a food processor or blender. Purée each batch with proportionate quantities of the reserved ⅓ cup of lemon juice and the sugar. This can be done in two to three batches in the food processor, or four to five batches in a blender. Be sure to divide the sugar and lemon juice equally between the batches. Force the purée through a strainer into a 1-quart measure. There should be about 3½ cups.

   Note: If you do not have a food processor or blender, combine the pears, lemon juice and sugar in a mixing bowl and mash with a pestle or potato masher. The pears must be puréed with both the lemon juice and sugar to keep them white, so a food mill does not work well for this.

4. Add enough water to the pear purée to make 4 cups, then add the *Poire Williams*. Stir to combine.

   Note: *Poire Williams* is quite strong; 1 tablespoon lends only a subtle hint of the alcohol, 2 tablespoons will add quite a distinctive flavor. Choose according to your taste.

5. Turn the mixture into the container of an ice cream machine or freezer, cover and freeze according to the manufacturer's instructions. (Some small, electric, freezer-model machines do not handle thick purée very well.) Or, place the purée in a metal tray or bowl, cover tightly and place in the freezer, periodically beating up the mixture as it freezes to break down the ice crystals.

   Note: To achieve a particularly smooth consistency if you have frozen the sherbet without a machine, cut it into chunks and purée until smooth in a food processor, then refreeze until ready to serve.

LEMON SHERBET IN LEMON SHELLS

Susan Lipke

6 servings

8 VERY LARGE, FIRM LEMONS,
  SCRUBBED
1 CUP SUGAR
LEMON LEAVES

1. Using a swivel action peeler, peel the rind—yellow zest only—from 1 of the lemons. Reserve the lemon. Cut the rind into fine julienne strips and blanch them for about 10 minutes in boiling water. Drain, dry on paper towels and reserve in a small bowl.

2. In a small saucepan, combine the sugar and ¼ cup of water and bring to a boil, swirling the pan until the sugar dissolves. Simmer just until it reaches the soft ball stage, about 225 F. on a candy thermometer. The syrup will be quite thick.

3. While the sugar syrup simmers, bring 1⅓ cups of water to a boil in another, larger pan.

4. Add 3 tablespoons of the sugar syrup to the julienned lemon rind and refrigerate.

5. Add some of the boiling water to the remaining sugar syrup, stir to blend, then add the warmed syrup to the rest of the boiling water. Set the pan in cold water to cool the syrup.

6. Using a fine-toothed grater or citrus zester, grate the rind (yellow zest only) of another of the lemons into a 1-cup measure. Set the grated rind and the lemon aside.

7. Arrange a fine-meshed strainer over a small bowl to catch the juice as you prepare the lemons. Using a short, sharp knife, peel the 2 reserved lemons over the strainer, removing (and discarding) every bit of the white rind, cutting right into the flesh of the fruit to do so.

8. Cut the sections from between the membranes and let the sections fall into the strainer. Squeeze the juice from any pulp left on the membranes into the strainer and then discard the membranes.

9. Carefully remove all of the seeds from the lemon sections in the strainer and then add the fruit to the grated rind in the measuring cup along with any strained juice in the bowl.

10. Shave a thin slice off the bottom (pointed end) of the 6 remaining lemons, so that they will sit upright on a flat surface. Slice the top third from each lemon and discard. Then, holding the lemons over the strainer, scoop out the pulp with a grapefruit knife or spoon. Cover the shells and place them in the freezer.

11. To the pulp in the measuring cup, add enough of the pulp and strained juice from the 6 lemons to make ⅔ cup all together. Make sure to remove any white membranes from the pulp. Mash the pulp with the back of a spoon to break it into smaller pieces.

    Note: There will be some lemon juice and pulp left over. Reserve it for other uses. or increase the quantities of water and sugar proportionately to make extra sherbet.

12. Add the lemon juice and pulp to the cooled sugar syrup and stir to combine. Turn into an ice cream machine and freeze according to manufacturer's instructions; or,

place in a metal tray or cake pan, cover and freeze, beating up the mixture from time to time to break down the ice crystals.

Note: If the sherbet gets too icy in spite of your best efforts, beat it until smooth in a food processor or blender.

13. When the sherbet is frozen firm but not solid, scoop it into the 6 lemon shells, mounding it 1″ to 2″ over the tops of the shells. Cover and return to the freezer.

14. If you have a deep freezer, place the lemons in the refrigerator about 30 minutes before serving, to soften.

15. When ready to serve, arrange the lemon leaves on six serving plates, place a lemon in the center of each and sprinkle a little of the candied peel over the sherbet.

Note: If you prefer, you may garnish the lemons with candied violets instead of candied peel. If so, it will not be necessary to make the sugar syrup. Reduce the quantity of sugar to ¾ cup and simply stir it until dissolved in the lemon juice and 1⅓ cups water.

STRAWBERRY SHERBET

Carol Cutler

8 servings

One of the big plusses for serving frozen sherbets and ice creams is that the busy cook can prepare them hours, even days before serving. But do try once preparing the dessert just an hour or two before serving, never allowing it to freeze completely. You will be spoiled for any other version.

½ CUP SUGAR
⅓ CUP WATER
1 QUART FRESH STRAWBERRIES
JUICE OF 1 LEMON
2 TABLESPOONS ORANGE LIQUEUR,
    PREFERABLY GRAND MARNIER
1 EGG WHITE

1. In a small, heavy pot, place the sugar and water and bring to a boil. Simmer for 5 minutes and remove from the heat; cool.

2. Hull and rinse the berries. Place them in the container of a blender with the lemon juice and orange liqueur and purée. There should be able 3 cups of purée.

3. Add the sugar syrup and blend again very briefly.

4. Lightly beat the egg white and pour it into the purée. Stir with a long spoon, but do not blend again.

5. Pour the strawberry mixture into the container of an ice cream freezer and freeze according to the manufacturer's instructions.

Note: If the sherbet is prepared a day or so in advance, remove it from the freezer about 15 minutes before serving.

PERSIMMON SHERBET

Emanuel and Madeline Greenberg *

4 to 6 servings

Since persimmons are a fall and winter fruit, this sherbet would be a fine light dessert after a substantial Thanksgiving or Christmas dinner.

1½ CUPS WATER
1 CUP SUGAR
2 MEDIUM-SIZED RIPE PERSIMMONS*
½ CUP YOGURT
3 TABLESPOONS LEMON JUICE
2 TABLESPOONS APRICOT-FLAVORED
  BRANDY

1. Bring the water and the sugar to a boil, stirring until the sugar dissolves. Boil for 5 minutes without stirring. Cool at room temperature.

2. Cut the persimmons in half and remove the seeds. Do this over a bowl to catch all of the juices. Scoop out the meat and drop it into a blender container, along with the juices; purée.

3. Measure out 1 cup of the purée and combine it with the yogurt, stirring until well blended and smooth. Add the cooled sugar syrup, lemon juice and apricot-flavored brandy.

4. Refrigerate about 1 hour. Pour into ice trays and place in the freezer. When the yogurt is frozen around the edges, but still soft in the center, turn it into a chilled bowl and beat until smooth. Pour back into the trays and freeze until firm.

5. If the sherbet is very hard frozen, transfer it to the refrigerator about 20 minutes before serving.

Note: The sherbet can also be made in an ice cream machine following the manufacturer's instructions.

*The persimmons must be absolutely ripe. The fruit should be soft, with a transparent skin. At its peak, it will look lush, even a bit wilted.

CHERRY JAM SHERBET

Jeanne Lesem

3 to 4 servings

I hit upon this idea while writing my preserving and pickling book. It's a good way to use up an oversupply of jam; but I also make it with good-quality commercial preserves. It's faster than cooking fruit with sugar, or even stirring raw fruit and sugar into a sherbet mixture.

⅔ CUP CHERRY JAM OR PRESERVES,
  APPROXIMATELY
1 TABLESPOON LEMON JUICE
2¼ CUPS MILK
2 TO 4 TABLESPOONS *KIRSCH*

1. Place the jam or preserves in a blender container or a food processor fitted with a steel blade. Process until almost smooth.

2. Place in an ice cream freezer can and stir in the lemon juice.

3. Stir in the milk and brandy and taste for sweetness, remembering that cold reduces sweetness. Add more processed jam or preserves, if desired, and stir to mix well.

   Note: Don't be alarmed if the milk curdles when you add the lemon juice. This will not affect the flavor or texture of the sherbet, and the appearance will be satisfactory once the mixture is frozen.

4. Freeze according to the manufacturer's instructions.

5. When the sherbet is frozen, remove the dasher and pack the sherbet down. Cover tightly and store in the freezer 2 to 3 hours, or overnight, to harden and mellow.

6. If the sherbet freezes too solidly, let it soften slightly in the refrigerator or at room temperature, then break it up with an electric handmixer until it is of serving consistency. Garnish with sliced fresh fruit before serving, or spoon a little additional *kirsch* over the sherbet for sauce.

Note: Other suggested combinations for this sherbet: damson plum jam or strawberry jam with *kirsch,* raspberry jam with peach brandy, or apple preserves with applejack or calvados.

PINEAPPLE SHERBET

Mireille Johnston

4 servings

This is a spectacular dessert. The ingredients are commonly available in most supermarkets, yet the four pineapple half-shells, served on a round platter like a giant flower, make an exotic and elegant dish.

1 CUP UNSWEETENED PINEAPPLE JUICE
1½ CUPS SUGAR
2 CUPS CRUSHED, UNSWEETENED,
  CANNED PINEAPPLE*
JUICE OF 1 VERY LARGE LEMON
1 TEASPOON SALT
2 SMALL PINEAPPLES
1 TABLESPOON DARK RUM OR *KIRSCH*
4 SPRIGS FRESH MINT (OPTIONAL)

1. Place the pineapple juice and sugar in a heavy-bottomed saucepan and boil for 5

Continued from preceding page

minutes, making certain that all of the sugar dissolves. Pour the syrup into a large bowl with the crushed pineapple, lemon juice and salt. Chill in the refrigerator.

2. Place the chilled mixture in the container of an ice cream machine and freeze until firm, according to the manufacturer's instructions.

3. Meanwhile, cut the fresh pineapples in half lengthwise and spoon out the pulp, leaving only ¼″ of the fruit attached to the shell.

4. Dice the pulp, sprinkle it with the rum or *kirsch* and set aside to macerate until the sherbet is ready, about 20 minutes.

5. Place the 4 pineapple half-shells in the middle of a large round serving platter, tops facing out. Spoon the sherbet into each of the four cavities and cover with the diced pineapple. Tuck a sprig of mint into each shell at the base of the pineapple. Serve with crunchy almond cookies and a sweet wine or a chilled white sparkling wine.

*If you can't buy already crushed, canned pineapple, crush the pineapple lightly with a fork. Do not purée it because it should have a coarse texture.

BANANA BUTTERMILK SHERBET

Elizabeth Schneider Colchie

1 quart

2 MEDIUM-SIZED, RIPE BANANAS
¾ CUP SUGAR
3 TABLEPOONS LEMON JUICE
LARGE PINCH OF NUTMEG
1 TEASPOON VANILLA EXTRACT
1 EGG, SEPARATED
LARGE PINCH OF SALT
2 CUPS BUTTERMILK

1. In a blender or food processor, purée the bananas with ½ cup sugar, the lemon juice and nutmeg. There should be about 1½ cups of purée.

2. In a medium-sized bowl, beat together the vanilla, egg yolk, salt and remaining ¼ cup sugar, until the mixture is pale.

3. Beat the banana purée into the egg mixture. Stir in the buttermilk.

4. In a small bowl, beat the egg white until stiff and fold it into the banana-buttermilk mixture.

5. Turn into a 1-quart ice cream maker and follow the manufacturer's instructions for freezing. Allow to soften slightly in the refrigerator before serving.

TOMATO-PEACH SHERBET

Jeanne Lesem

1 quart

The idea for this sherbet came from my collection of 19th-century preserving and pickling books. Because jam made from the two fruits was so good, I decided to try the combination for sherbet.

1 POUND RIPE TOMATOES
1 POUND RIPE PEACHES
½ CUP WATER
¾ CUP SUGAR (OR MORE, TO TASTE)
1 TEASPOON VANILLA EXTRACT
1 CUP MILK

1. Peel, core and slice the tomatoes.

2. Peel, pit and slice the peaches.

3. In a 2-quart saucepan, combine the tomato and peach slices with the water. Bring the water and fruit to a boil over high heat and boil rapidly, stirring occasionally, for about 20 minutes, or until the peaches are tender and the tomatoes broken up.

4. Remove the fruit from the heat, cool slightly, and purée in a food mill. There should be about 2½ cups of the purée.

5. Stir in the sugar until no crystals remain, then stir in the vanilla, cover and refrigerate until well chilled—a few hours or overnight.

6. When you are ready to freeze the sherbet, taste the chilled mixture and add more sugar if desired, remembering that cold mutes the sweetness of the sherbet. Stir in the milk, blending thoroughly.

   Note: Do not be alarmed if the acid in the tomato curdles the milk. It will not affect the end result.

7. Pour the mixture into the container of an electric or hand-cranked freezer, insert the dasher, cover tightly and freeze according to the manufacturer's instructions.

8. When the sherbet is frozen, remove the dasher, pack the sherbet down, cover tightly, and place in the freezer to mellow for a few hours.

Note: Because of its low sugar content, the sherbet may freeze too hard in a zero-degree freezer unit. If so, remove it to the refrigerator for about 15 minutes before serving, to soften it slightly. If necessary, break it up with an electric mixer until it is of serving consistency.

Ices and Granite

GRAPEFRUIT, ORANGE AND LEMON ICE

Nan Mabon

6 servings

As a New Yorker, one of my favorite shopping and eating haunts is the Little Italy section in lower Manhattan. Every spring I look forward to the arrival of Italian ices in the little cafes that line the streets there. I've now learned to make my own in a food processor or blender.

2 CUPS WATER
1 CUP SUGAR
GRATED RIND OF ½ GRAPEFRUIT
GRATED RIND OF 1 ORANGE
GRATED RIND OF 1 LEMON
1 CUP FRESHLY-SQUEEZED GRAPEFRUIT
   JUICE
1 CUP FRESHLY-SQUEEZED ORANGE
   JUICE
½ CUP FRESHLY-SQUEEZED LEMON
   JUICE

1. Put the water and sugar in a saucepan and dissolve the sugar over medium heat. Bring to a boil and let simmer for 5 minutes; cool.

2. Combine and mix the sugar syrup, grated rinds and fruit juices. Pour this mixture into ice trays (dividers removed) and freeze for several hours or overnight.

3. When the mixture is solidly frozen, place half in the bowl of a food processor or blender. Process until the ice is smooth and free of lumps. Repeat with the other half of the frozen mixture.

   Note: This can also be made in an ice cream freezer. Pour the unfrozen mixture directly into the freezer container and freeze according to the manufacturer's instructions.

4. Store the processed ice in a covered container in the freezer for a few hours before serving. This is a wonderful finish to a rich, heavy meal.

5. Serve in iced glass bowls and garnish them with paper-thin slices of lemon, orange and grapefruit.

GINNED CRANBERRY ICE

Michael Batterberry

12 to 16 servings

6 CUPS (ONE 15-OUNCE BAG) FRESH
   CRANBERRIES
3 CUPS WATER
2¼ CUPS SUGAR
1 JAR (10 OUNCES) SEEDLESS RASP-
   BERRY PRESERVES
½ CUP FRESH ORANGE JUICE
½ CUP GIN
TINY PINCH OF SALT

1. Place the cranberries and water in an enameled or heatproof glass saucepan and bring to a boil. Simmer until the skins begin to pop, about 4 to 5 minutes.

2. Add the sugar and raspberry preserves and simmer, stirring constantly, another 7 to 8 minutes. Skim off any scum that may accumulate, then add the orange juice, gin and salt.

3. Cool, then place the mixture in the freezer and freeze, beating occasionally to break up the ice crystals.

   Note: The ice may also be frozen in an ice cream machine.

4. Serve in scoops or in small orange shell halves, not only as a dessert, but as a splendid accompaniment to game, pork or roast turkey.

Note: This extremely authoritative and tart *sorbet* is properly best served in small portions.

COFFEE GRANITA

Emanuel and Madeline Greenberg

6 to 8 servings

1 CUP WATER
¾ CUP SUGAR
ONE 2″-LONG STICK CINNAMON
ONE 2″-LONG STRIP LEMON PEEL
   (YELLOW PART ONLY)
3 CUPS DOUBLE STRENGTH OR
   ESPRESSO COFFEE, CHILLED

1. In a saucepan, combine the water, the sugar, cinnamon stick and lemon peel. Bring to a boil, stirring until the sugar dissolves. Boil 5 minutes without stirring. Remove and discard the cinnamon stick and lemon peel. Cool the syrup at room temperature.

2. Combine the cooled syrup with the coffee. Refrigerate about 1 hour.

3. Pour into ice trays and place in the freezer. Stir well every 30 minutes, until firm.

4. Served as is, the *granite* makes a refreshing substitute for dessert and coffee.

Continued from preceding page

For an extra fillip, combine 2 parts heavy cream with 1 part Amaretto, *crème de cacao* or coffee liqueur and pour some over each serving.

Note: If the *granite* freezes too hard, break it up and whirl in a blender for a few seconds.

FRESH MINT-TEA ICE

Elizabeth Schneider Colchie

1 quart

⅔ CUP SUGAR
2½ CUPS COLD WATER
¾ CUP LOOSELY-PACKED, CHOPPED
   FRESH MINT
1½ CUPS BOILING WATER
2 TABLESPOONS STRONG BLACK TEA
   LEAVES
MINT LEAVES

1. Bring the sugar and water to a boil, stirring. Add the mint and boil for 5 minutes.

2. Pour the boiling water over the tea leaves and let steep 5 minutes. Strain into a bowl. Strain in the mint infusion. Let cool.

3. Pour the mixture into a cake pan or ice trays and freeze until almost hard. Scoop into the bowl of an electric mixer and beat for a minute or two.

4. Return to the cake pan or ice trays and freeze again until almost firm. Beat up the crystals once again.

5. Cover the bowl with plastic wrap or foil and freeze for 12 hours, or more, before serving.

6. Garnish with tiny mint leaves before serving.

Note: If the mixture gets too solid, or you desire an even finer, snowier texture, you may beat up the mixture a third time before storing. The ice will keep for 4 to 5 days.

BLACK GRAPE ICE

Paula Wolfert

6 servings

1 POUND BLACK GRAPES
1 CUP SUGAR
½ CUP WATER
JUICE OF 2 LEMONS
¼ CUP RUBY PORT WINE
WHIPPED CREAM

1. The day before you plan to serve the ice, purée the grapes in a blender and push them through a sieve to remove the skins and pips.

2. In a saucepan, combine the sugar and water and cook, stirring, over medium heat, until the sugar dissolves. Boil the syrup for 5 minutes. Pour into a mixing bowl and allow to cool.

3. Stir in the grape purée and the lemon juice. Whisk until well blended.

4. Pour the grape mixture into 6-cup mold and set in the freezer compartment until the mixture is mushy but set around the rim of the mold.

5. Using an electric beater, beat the frozen mush until smooth. Return to the freezer and freeze overnight.

6. Remove from the freezer, beat again, add the port wine, and refreeze until firm.

7. Turn out onto a serving dish and serve with a small bowl of whipped cream.

MELON SUPREME ICE

Michael Batterberry

8 to 12 servings

2 RIPE, MEDIUM-SIZED CANTALOUPES
2½ LIMES
2 TABLESPOONS COINTREAU
2 CUPS SAUTERNE
¾ CUP SUGAR
TINY PINCH OF SALT
1 TABLESPOON FINELY CHOPPED
   CANDIED GINGER

1. In a blender and in two or more batches, smoothly purée the meat of the melon with a squeeze or two of lime juice, the Cointreau and as much sauterne as necessary to keep the blender spinning freely.

   Note: A food processor will not present this problem.

2. In a saucepan, over low heat, dissolve the sugar completely in the remaining sauterne. Let cool.

3. In a metal bowl, combine the syrup with the puréed fruit. Stir in the salt and candied ginger, then place the bowl in the freezer. As the mixture freezes, beat it occasionally to break up the ice crystals.

   Note: The ice may also be frozen in an ice cream machine.

4. After the last beating, when it is smooth and fairly well frozen, pack the ice into a decorative ring mold and return it to the freezer. Unmold just before serving.

Note: Melon supreme is particularly glamorous when decorated with strips of fresh kumquats, with their glossy green leaves, and cubed fresh pineapple, sweetened if desired, and marinated in a little *kirschwasser* or *framboise*.

41

Frozen Cakes, Pies and Concoctions

SPONGE ROLL WITH LIGHT CHOCOLATE MOUSSE

Isabel S. Cornell

8 servings

Light Chocolate Mousse:
1 ENVELOPE UNFLAVORED GELATIN
¼ CUP STRONG COFFEE OR WATER
2 EGG YOLKS
1 PACKAGE (6 OUNCES) SEMISWEET
   CHOCOLATE BITS
1¼ CUPS LIGHT CREAM, HEATED
⅓ CUP SUGAR
1 TEASPOON VANILLA EXTRACT
2 TABLESPOONS *CRÈME DE CACAO*
1 TABLESPOON *CRÈME DE MENTHE*
1 CUP HEAVY CREAM, WHIPPED

Sponge-Cake Roll:
4 EGGS, SEPARATED
1 CUP SUGAR
1 TEASPOON VANILLA EXTRACT
1 CUP SIFTED FLOUR
1 TEASPOON BAKING POWDER
⅛ TEASPOON SALT
3 TABLESPOONS WATER

1. Soak the gelatin in the cool coffee or water.

2. Put the gelatin into a blender container with the egg yolks and chocolate bits. (Do *not* blend yet.)

3. Slowly pour some of the hot cream into the blender, turn it on and finish adding the cream while it is running. Blend until smooth.

4. Blend in the sugar, vanilla and liqueurs.

5. Chill the mixture until it begins to thicken; then fold in 1½ cups of the whipped cream. Reserve the remainder for garnish.

6. Chill while preparing the cake. The mousse should become firm enough to spread without running. Put it in the freezer to hasten the process, if necessary.

7. Preheat the oven to 350 F.

8. Beat the egg whites until they just hold a peak; gradually beat in ½ cup sugar, 1 tablespoon at a time. Keep beating until the egg whites are stiff and glossy.

9. Beat the egg yolks well; beat in the vanilla and the remaining ½ cup sugar, and continue beating until light colored and fluffy.

10. Fold in the beaten whites.

11. Sift the flour, baking powder and salt together; fold into the batter alternately with the water.

12. Line a 10"x15" jelly-roll pan with foil and grease well. Pour in the batter, smooth the top, and bake in the preheated oven for 15 to 17 minutes, or until the top of the cake springs back when pressed with a finger.

13. Carefully turn the cake out on a damp towel sprinkled with sugar; remove the foil and trim off any crisp edges. Starting at the narrow end, quickly roll up the cake in the towel and let it cool to room temperature.

14. When the mousse is firm, unroll the cake and spread it with the filling. Quickly reroll and wrap it in foil and freeze.

15. About 30 minutes before serving time, remove to the refrigerator to partially thaw. Slice, and serve with the remaining whipped cream.

FROZEN MAPLE SOUFFLÉ
(SOUFFLÉ GLACÉE À L'ÉRABLE

Carol Cutler

10 servings

Rich though this dessert might be, the crisp flavor of the maple guarantees a fresh note for a meal's finale.

4 EGGS
1 CUP PURE MAPLE SYRUP
1¼ CUPS WHIPPING CREAM
1 TEASPOON MAPLE FLAVORING
1½ TABLESPOONS DARK RUM
PINCH OF CREAM OF TARTAR

1. Separate the eggs, putting the yolks in a small, heavy pot and the whites in a mixing bowl.

2. Beat the yolks until light, then add the maple syrup. Put the pot over low heat, and warm the syrup just until the liquid is hot to the touch. Do not overcook.

3. Meanwhile—keeping an eye on the syrup—whip 1 cup of the cream until firm.

4. When the syrup is hot, remove it at once from the heat and stir in the maple flavoring and rum. Transfer to a large mixing bowl.

5. Beat the syrup mixture until it is light and frothy, then fold in the whipped cream.

6. Add the cream of tartar to the egg whites and beat until firm. Fold the beaten whites into the syrup-cream mixture, one half at a time.

7. Attach a collar to an 8-cup soufflé mold. Turn the soufflé into the mold, smooth the top and freeze.

8. Remove the soufflé from the freezer 10 minutes before serving; remove the collar.

9. Beat the remaining whipping cream and pipe it through a pastry tube to decorate the top of the soufflé before serving.

MERINGUE TIMBALE (VACHERIN)

Alma Lach

One 8" cake

A *timbale* is a container in which food is served and/or cooked. In this case, layers of cooked meringue are used to create an impressive, decorative and very edible container for ice cream or whipped cream and fruits.

12 LARGE EGGS
VINEGAR
¾ TEASPOON SALT
¾ TEASPOON CREAM OF TARTAR
3 CUPS SUPERFINE SUGAR
ICE CREAM

1. Separate 8 of the eggs; reserve the yolks for another use.

2. Wipe a large mixer bowl with a small amount of vinegar. Add the egg whites and then, beating on low speed, add ½ teaspoon of the salt. Beat on low speed for about 2 minutes. Add ½ teaspoon of the cream of tartar and increase the speed to medium; beat for 1 minute. When big bubbles give way to tiny ones, gradually add 4 tablespoons of sugar and increase the speed to high, but not top speed.

3. Once the egg whites are creamy and starting to stiffen, gradually add 1¾ cups sugar and continue to beat until the whites are glossy and thick.

4. Put a little more than half of the meringue into a large pastry bag fitted with a ½" plain nozzle. Refrigerate the remainder of the meringue.

5. Preheat the oven to 225 F.

6. Butter and flour two cookie sheets. With an 8"-diameter cake pan, mark four circles on the floured sheets.

   Note: To fit two 8" circles on a standard-sized cookie sheet, mark the circles in opposite corners.

7. Staying just inside the circumference, pipe a 1"-wide band of meringue in each of the four circles. Then, evenly fill in the center of only one of the circles.

8. Bake the meringues in the preheated oven for about 1 hour, or until they are are dried out but not browned.

9. Remove the meringues from the oven, but leave the temperature set at 225 F. Cool the meringues on the cookie sheets and then transfer them very carefully to a flat surface.

10. Wash one of the two cookie sheets, and cover it with a sheet of aluminum foil. Place the solid layer of baked meringue in the middle of the sheet.

11. Fill the pastry bag, fitted with the ½" plain nozzle, with the remaining, refrigerated meringue. Pipe a band of meringue around the upper edge of the baked layer. Place one of the cooked rings on top. Pipe another band of meringue on the cooked ring and place the second ring on top of that. Repeat for the third ring.

    Note; If there is any meringue left in the bag, fill in any cracks on the sides of the *timbale.*

12. Bake the *timbale* in the 225 F. oven for 45 to 60 minutes, or until the merin-

gue is dried out. Remove from the oven and allow to cool. Leave the oven set at 225 F.

13. While the *timbale* is cooling, make another batch of meringue. Separate the remaining 4 eggs (reserve the yolks for another use). Beat the whites in the same manner as described in Steps 2 and 3, adding the remaining ¼ teaspoon of salt, ¼ teaspoon cream of tartar and 1 cup of sugar.

14. Divide the meringue in half. Use one half to "frost" the outside of the cool *timbale* to make it smooth. Place the remaining half of the meringue in a pastry bag fitted with a star nozzle, and pipe fancy decorations on the smoothed sides of the *timbale*. On the top ring of the *timbale*, pipe stars or flute a ribbon.

15. Place the decorated *timbale* back in the 225 F. oven for about 1 hour, or until completely dry. Allow to cool.

16. To serve, fill the center of the *timbale* with assorted ice cream balls. Whipped cream and fresh fruit make a lovely alternative filling.

Note: The foundation rings of the *timbale* can be made days in advance and kept dry by storing them in an oven heated by a pilot light.

FROZEN PUMPKIN PIE

Carol Cutler

8 to 10 servings

Crust:
1½ CUPS GRAHAM CRACKER CRUMBS
¼ CUP SUGAR
4 TABLESPOONS (½ STICK) BUTTER,
  MELTED

Filling:
1 TO 1½ CUPS COOKED PUMPKIN,
  FRESH OR CANNED

½ CUP BROWN SUGAR
½ TEASPOON SALT
1 TEASPOON CINNAMON
⅛ TEASPOON GROUND CLOVES
1 QUART VANILLA ICE CREAM,
  SOFTENED
½ CUP HEAVY CREAM, WHIPPED
  (OPTIONAL)
¼ CUP PECANS (OPTIONAL)

1. Mix together the graham cracker crumbs, sugar and melted butter. Press into an 8" pie pan and chill for at least 30 minutes.

2. Combine the pumpkin, sugar and all the spices.

3. Fold the pumpkin mixture into the softened ice cream. Fill the chilled pie shell and freeze until firm.

4. Remove from the freezer 30 minutes before serving. Garnish, if desired, with whipped cream and pecans.

Note: For another presentation of this exceptional pie, press the graham cracker crumb mixture into the bottom of a 9" square pan. Proceed as above for the filling and freeze. At serving time, cut into squares.

MAPLE PARFAIT

Raymond Sokolov

4 to 6 servings

4 EGG YOLKS
½ CUP MAPLE SYRUP
¼ TEASPOON SALT
½ TEASPOON VANILLA EXTRACT
1½ CUPS HEAVY CREAM, WHIPPED
¼ CUP CHOPPED NUTS OR ⅓ CUP
   CRUSHED NUT BRITTLE (OPTIONAL)

1. In the top of a 1½-quart double boiler, beat the egg yolks.

2. Add the maple syrup and salt and cook over simmering water, beating with a rotary beater until the mixture is thick and fluffy.

3. Add the vanilla, set in a pan of ice water and continue beating until cold.

4. Fold in the whipped cream and nuts or nut brittle, if desired.

5. Turn into a 1-quart mold or freezer tray and freeze as quickly as possible. Set the freezer temperature control at its coldest point.

6. Serve plain or with maple syrup and nuts.

SURPRISE DESSERT CRÊPES

Paul Rubinstein

6 servings

2 TEASPOONS MELTED BUTTER
1 CUP SIFTED FLOUR
¼ TEASPOON SALT
2 EGGS
1½ CUPS MILK
1 TABLESPOON CONFECTIONERS'
   SUGAR

SOFTENED BUTTER
2 CUPS APRICOT JAM OR PRESERVES
⅔ CUP WATER
3 TABLESPOONS GRANULATED SUGAR
2 TABLESPOONS COINTREAU OR
   BRANDY
3 PINTS FRENCH VANILLA ICE CREAM

1. In a mixing bowl, combine the melted butter, flour, salt, eggs, milk and confectioners' sugar. Beat with an electric mixer until smooth.

2. Heat the oven to 200 F. and place a round, ovenproof glass pie dish in it to warm.

3. Heat a 7" to 8" crêpe pan over medium-high heat. Add about 1 teaspoon softened butter, then 2 tablespoons of the crêpe batter to the pan. Immediately tilt the pan around to allow the batter to spread evenly over the bottom. Cook until the edges begin to brown. Flip the crêpe over with a thin spatula and cook on the other side for a few seconds, until lightly browned (check by lifting the edge to look at the bottom).

4. Transfer the cooked crêpe to the dish in the warm oven and repeat until the batter is used up. There should be over a dozen thin crêpes.

5. In a small saucepan, combine the apricot jam and water and granulated sugar. Stir over medium heat until the mixture comes to a simmer; reduce the heat and cook 5 minutes, stirring occasionally.

6. Add the Cointreau, stir and keep the sauce warm over very low heat.

7. Assemble the crêpes just before serving: Lay a warm crêpe on a board or other flat surface. With an ice cream scoop or shovel, measure out a portion of about ¼ pint (½ cup) of ice cream and place it on the crêpe. If possible, use an ice cream spade and make an oblong-shaped piece of ice cream rather than a spherical scoop. Roll up the crêpe and place it on a serving platter. Continue until 12 crêpes have been rolled, keeping in mind that it is important to work as fast as possible.

8. Spoon the hot apricot over the crêpes and serve immediately, allowing 2 crêpes per person.

FROZEN ORANGE SOUFFLÉ

Maria Luisa Scott and Jack Denton Scott

8 servings

1 TABLESPOON (1 ENVELOPE) UNFLA-VORED GELATIN
¼ CUP COLD WATER
3 EGGS, SEPARATED
½ CUP SUGAR
¼ CUP FROZEN ORANGE JUICE CONCENTRATE, THAWED

2 TABLESPOONS LEMON JUICE
½ TEASPOON GRATED ORANGE RIND
½ TEASPOON GRATED LEMON RIND
2 TABLESPOONS GRAND MARNIER
2 CUPS HEAVY CREAM, WHIPPED
FRESH, WELL-DRAINED ORANGE SECTIONS

1. Soak the gelatin in the cold water (it will more or less solidify).

2. In a large bowl, beat the egg yolks until lemon colored and light. Gradually add the sugar, beating constantly. Beat until fluffy.

3. Beat in the orange juice concentrate, lemon juice, orange and lemon rinds and the Grand Marnier.

4. Heat the gelatin over hot water and stir until it is clear and liquid. Add this to the egg yolk mixture and mix well.

5. Refrigerate until the mixture starts to set, about 10 or 15 minutes.

6. While the gelatin-egg yolk mixture is in the refrigerator, beat the egg whites until stiff.

7. Remove the gelatin mixture from the refigerator when it starts to set and fold in first the beaten cream, then the egg whites.

8. Spoon into individual soufflé dishes, or into one large soufflé dish with a collar, and freeze.

9. Remove from the freezer 30 minutes before serving, remove the collar and garnish with the orange sections.

BAKED ALASKA

Dorothy Parker

8 to 10 servings

Cake:
4 EGGS, SEPARATED
1 CUP SUGAR
4 TEASPOONS COLD LEMON JUICE
1½ TEASPOONS GRATED LEMON RIND
1 CUP FLOUR
⅛ TEASPOON BAKING SODA

Meringue:
4 EGG WHITES

⅛ TEASPOON CREAM OF TARTAR
¾ CUP SUGAR

Other Ingredients:
1 QUART ICE CREAM, FROZEN HARD*
CONFECTIONERS' SUGAR (OPTIONAL)

1. Preheat the oven to 350 F.
2. Lightly grease and flour two 8″ or 9″ round cake tins.
3. Beat the egg yolks until fluffy, adding ½ cup of the sugar gradually. While beating, stir in the lemon juice and rind.
4. Sift the flour with the baking soda, then stir into the egg yolk mixture.
5. Beat the egg whites until they form soft peaks. Add the remaining ½ cup of sugar and continue beating until the meringue forms stiff, glossy peaks. Fold this meringue into the cake batter.
6. Turn half of the batter into each of the prepared pans. Bake for 30 minutes in the preheated oven. Test for doneness. Allow to cool completely.
7. Select a baking dish somewhat longer than the cakes and place one of the layers on it. Top with a 1″-thick layer of ice cream slightly smaller than the dimensions of the cake. Place a second layer on top of the ice cream, and then add one more ice cream layer.

   Note: If the ice cream is in brick form, trim the cake layers to make them square.

8. Freeze the layered cake and ice cream until ready to serve.
9. Preheat the over to 475 F.
10. Into a mixing bowl or blender jar, place the 4 egg whites and the baking soda (or cream of tartar). Beat to the soft-peak stage, then add the sugar, a little at a time, and continue beating until the whites are quite stiff.
11. Cover the construction on the top and all sides with the stiff meringue, working fast and making sure that no opening remains in the meringue. Dust the surface of the meringue with confectioners' sugar, if desired.

    Note: The meringue must form an airtight insulation for the ice cream, or the results will be disastrous.

12. Place the dessert into the preheated oven for no longer than it takes to turn the meringue golden, about 3 to 5 minutes.
13. Serve the Baked Alaska immediately, as is.

*Use a three-colored brick or *spumone;* or use plain chocolate, strawberry or other plain ice cream that offers a contrasting color to the cake.

ICE CREAM MOLD WITH STRAWBERRY FILLING
(BOMBE COMTESSE-MARIE)

Alma Lach

8 servings

Technically, this should be made in a Comtesse-Marie mold, which is square with fluted designs in the bottom. However, any 2-quart ice cream mold can be substituted.

1 QUART RICH VANILLA ICE CREAM
1 QUART STRAWBERRIES
½ CUP SUGAR
1 TABLESPOON CALVADOS
2 TEASPOONS *KIRSCH*
1 TEASPOON UNFLAVORED GELATIN
1 CUP WHIPPING CREAM
3 TABLESPOONS CONFECTIONERS'
   SUGAR
½ TEASPOON VANILLA EXTRACT

1. Place the ice cream mold *in* the freezer, and take the ice cream *out* of the freezer to soften.

2. Once the ice cream is workable, line the frozen mold with a 1″ layer, working as quickly as possible. This should use all of the ice cream.

3. Press a sheet of aluminum foil into the mold to hold the ice cream in place and place the mold back in the freezer to harden.

4. Meanwhile, prepare the strawberries. Wash and hull them and set aside four whole berries to decorate the mold. Cut the remaining strawberries into lengthwise slices.

5. Place the strawberry slices in a bowl with the sugar, calvados and *kirsch*. Toss to cover the berries and place in the refrigerator to macerate until the ice cream is frozen solid.

6. Drain the berries and reserve the liquid.

7. In a small, heavy saucepan, soften the gelatin in 1 tablespoon of the reserved liquid; dissolve the gelatin over very low heat. Stir into the drained berries.

8. Whip the cream with the confectioners' sugar and vanilla, and then fold into the berries.

9. Remove the ice cream mold from the freezer and remove the foil. Fill the cavity with the strawberry-whipped cream mixture. Cover with foil and freeze.

   Note: The mold may not quite hold all of the filling. To take care of the surplus, rinse one or more small molds with cold water, fill with the extra mixture and freeze.

10. To serve, unmold and pipe rosettes of whipped cream on each corner, if desired. Top each rosette with a whole strawberry.

FROZEN FRUIT TORTE

Paul Rubinstein

6 servings

This recipe combines fresh fruits with softened ice cream, which are built into a multi-layered torte. The procedure is quite simple, as long as plenty of time is allowed for the freezing of each layer before the next is added. A springform pan is essential.

2 CUPS HEAVY CREAM
1 PINT VANILLA ICE CREAM
1 TABLESPOON *FRAMBOISE* OR
  KIRSCH BRANDY
½ CUP FRESH RASPBERRIES
1 PINT CHOCOLATE ICE CREAM
½ CUP SLICED BANANAS
1 PINT COFFEE ICE CREAM
½ CUP GOOSEBERRY PRESERVES
6 MARASCHINO CHERRIES

1. With an electric mixer, whip the heavy cream until it forms stiff peaks. Score a cross in the surface of the cream to indicate roughly four equal portions, and refrigerate.

2. Allow the vanilla ice cream to soften at room temperature until it achieves a semi-liquid state.

3. Pour the brandy over the raspberries in a bowl and let them stand.

4. In a bowl, fold together one-quarter of the whipped cream, the softened vanilla ice cream and the raspberries. Pour the mixture into the bottom of an 8" to 9" round springform pan, 2½" to 3" deep, and freeze.

5. Take out the chocolate ice cream to soften.

6. Just as for the vanilla ice cream, fold together the softened chocolate ice cream with another one-quarter of the whipped cream and the banana.

7. When the raspberry-vanilla layer has frozen, add the chocolate layer to the pan and freeze.

8. Take out the coffee ice cream to soften.

9. Combine the softened ice cream, one-quarter of the whipped cream and the gooseberry preserves, and make the third layer when the chocolate layer is hardened. Freeze again.

10. Just before serving, unmold the torte from the springform and transfer it to a serving platter or cake plate. Decorate the torte with the remaining whipped cream (piped through a pastry bag fitted with a decorative nozzle) and the cherries.

11. Serve immediately, cutting into wedges at the table.

PINEAPPLE-RUM BOMBE

Dorothy Parker

8 to 10 servings

FLAVORLESS VEGETABLE OIL
1 QUART HARD-FROZEN VANILLA ICE
  CREAM, APPROXIMATELY
2½ CUPS SUGAR
1½ CUPS WATER
6 OR 7 MEDIUM-SIZED EGG YOLKS
¼ CUP RUM
1 CUP CANNED CRUSHED PINEAPPLE,
  DRAINED
1½ CUPS HEAVY CREAM
PECANS OR SLICED ALMONDS

1. Chill a 2-quart ice cream *bombe* mold severely; then brush it very lightly with vegetable oil. Line the mold with a 1''-thick layer of ice cream, packing it in hard. Place the mold in the freezer and chill for at least 30 minutes.

2. Meanwhile, in the top of a double boiler, combine the sugar and water. Cook it over low heat until it forms a thick syrup.

3. Put the egg yolks in a blender jar and blend on low speed until fluffy. Turn to a high speed and add the warm syrup, a little at a time, to the yolks. Continue beating at high speed until the custard is cool and creamy.

4. Combine the rum and drained, crushed pineapple. Stir into the cool custard, blending well.

5. Put into the refrigerator (*not* the freezer) for 30 minutes, or until well chilled.

6. Whip the cream until it is quite stiff, but not dry. Fold it into the chilled fruit custard. Distribute it well without disturbing the ice cream shell.

7. Remove the mold from the freezer. Fill the frozen ice cream shell with the egg-pineapple-whipped cream mixture.

8. Cover the mold and put it in the freezer. Freeze for at least 5 hours.

9. Remove the mold from the freezer 5 to 7 minutes before serving. Dip it into warm water for an instant, remove the lid and turn the *bombe* out onto a serving plate or board. Garnish with sliced nuts.

STRAWBERRY CURRANT PARFAIT

Isabel S. Cornell

8 servings

1 PACKAGE (16 OUNCES) FROZEN
  STRAWBERRIES, THAWED*
2 TABLESPOONS *CRÈME DE CASSIS*
2 TABLESPOONS BRANDY
2 CUPS PINEAPPLE OR VANILLA ICE
  CREAM
1 CUP LEMON OR PINEAPPLE SHERBET
1 CUP HEAVY CREAM, WHIPPED
PISTACHIO NUTS, CHOPPED

1. Drain the juice from the berries and reserve.

2. Mix the berries with the *crème de cassis* and brandy and let stand a few minutes.

3. Soften the ice cream and sherbet at room temperature just until they can be stirred together with the berries, liqueur and ¼ cup of the reserved juice.

4. Reserve ¼ cup of the whipped cream for topping and fold the rest into the ice cream-sherbert mixture.

5. Divide the parfait among eight glasses, top each with a heaping teaspoonful of whipped cream and sprinkle with pistachio nuts.

6. Place in the freezer; then, 1 hour before serving time, set them in the refrigerator to partially thaw.

*To use fresh strawberries, thinly slice about 3 cups of berries, sweeten to taste and let stand about ½ hour to develop juice.

BAKED ORANGE ALASKA

Bianca Brown

4 servings

½ CUP CHOPPED CANDIED FRUITS
¼ CUP PLUS 1 TABLESPOON ORANGE-
  FLAVORED LIQUEUR
4 MEDIUM-SIZED ORANGES
2 PINTS ORANGE SHERBET
2 EGG WHITES
PINCH OF SALT
SUPERFINE OR QUICK-DISSOLVING
  SUGAR

1. In a small bowl, macerate the candied fruits in the ¼ cup orange liqueur for at least 1 hour.

2. With a sharp knife, cut off the top quarter, and a very thin slice from the bottom, of

each orange.

3. With a grapefruit knife, remove the pulp, then scrape any remaining pulp from the shells with a spoon. Reserve the pulp for another use. Freeze the shells for 30 minutes.

4. Fill the orange shells one-third full with the orange sherbet. Spoon a tablespoon of the candied fruits with a little of the liqueur over the sherbet. Make another layer of sherbet, top with the rest of the candied fruits and cover with the remaining sherbet. Freeze the filled orange shells for several hours.

Note: Depending on the size of the oranges, there may be a little sherbet left over.

5. Preheat the oven to 450 F.

6. In a bowl, beat the egg whites with a pinch of salt until foamy. Gradually beat in 2 tablespoons of sugar and the remaining tablespoon of orange liqueur, and continue beating the whites until they hold stiff, but not dry, peaks.

7. Mound the upper portions of the filled orange shells with the meringue, covering the sherbet completely. Sprinkle the meringue lightly with sugar.

8. Set the oranges on a wooden board or a baking sheet and bake them for 3 to 5 minutes, or until the meringue is lightly browned. Serve immediately.

CHOCOLATE MOUSSE CAKE

Maria Luisa Scott and Jack Denton Scott

6 to 8 servings

24 LADYFINGERS, SPLIT LENGTHWISE
  BUT NOT SEPARATED
⅓ CUP PLUS 2 TABLESPOONS WHITE
  RUM
12 OUNCES SEMISWEET CHOCOLATE
5 EGGS, SEPARATED
¼ CUP SUPERFINE SUGAR
1 TEASPOON VANILLA EXTRACT
3 TABLESPOONS STRONG COFFEE
1½ CUPS HEAVY CREAM, WHIPPED
½ CUP COARSELY CHOPPED HAZELNUTS

1. Brush the flat sides of the ladyfingers with ⅓ cup of the white rum and, with their flat sides against the pan, line the sides and bottom of an 8″ springform mold.

2. In the top of a double boiler, melt the chocolate over hot water, stirring until smooth. Set aside.

3. In a large bowl, beat the egg whites until stiff. Gradually add 2 tablespoons of sugar, beating until stiff peaks form. Set aside.

4. In a separate large bowl, beat the egg yolks at high speed until foamy. Gradually beat in the remaining 2 tablespoons sugar, beating until light. Reduce the speed and beat in the remaining 2 tablespoons of rum, the vanilla and coffee.

5. Fold 1 cup of the egg whites into the chocolate to lighten it.

Continued from preceding page

6. Fold the chocolate-egg white mixture into the egg yolks, then fold in the remaining egg whites. Finally, fold in the whipped cream.

7. Pour the mousse into the lined mold. Sprinkle the top with the nuts.

8. Freeze until firm. Remove from the freezer 30 minutes before serving and remove the outside ring from the springform pan.